Teaching Playwriting

Teaching Playwriting

Creativity in Practice

Paul Gardiner

methuen | drama

LONDON • NEW YORK • OXFORD • NEW DELHI • SYDNEY

METHUEN DRAMA
Bloomsbury Publishing Plc
50 Bedford Square, London, WC1B 3DP, UK
1385 Broadway, New York, NY 10018, USA

BLOOMSBURY, METHUEN DRAMA and the Methuen Drama logo are
trademarks of Bloomsbury Publishing Plc

First published in Great Britain 2019

Cover design by Avni Patel

A catalogue record for this book is available from the British Library.

Library of Congress Cataloging-in-Publication Data
Names: Gardiner, Paul, author.
Title: Teaching playwriting: theory in practice / Paul Gardiner.
Description: London, UK; New York, NY: Methuen Drama, 2019. |
Includes bibliographical references.
Identifiers: LCCN 2018042453 | ISBN 9781350011328 (hb) |
ISBN 9781474288019 (pb) | ISBN 9781474288026 (ePDF) |
ISBN 9781474288033 (eBook)
Subjects: LCSH: Playwriting–Study and teaching.
Classification: LCC PN1661 .G35 2019 | DDC 808.2–dc23
LC record available at https://lccn.loc.gov/2018042453

ISBN: HB: 978-1-3500-1132-8
PB: 978-1-4742-8801-9
ePDF: 978-1-4742-8802-6
eBook: 978-1-4742-8803-3

Typeset by Deanta Global Publishing Services, Chennai, India
Printed and bound in Great Britain

To find out more about our authors and books visit www.bloomsbury.com
and sign up for our newsletters.

CONTENTS

ACKNOWLEDGEMENTS

I would like to thank the playwrights who agreed to be interviewed for this book and who offered their insights into the teaching of playwriting with such wisdom and generosity – Vanessa Bates, Hilary Bell, Lachlan Philpott, Polly Stenham and Simon Stephens. Their energy and passion for their craft was matched by their willingness to, as Simon called it, 'pass it on'.

I need to also thank the many students and teachers who were part of my research for their generosity and honesty.

I would like to thank the many students, past and present, whose love of drama continue to inspire me and whose honest and precise feedback on many of the activities included in this book has helped me refine and develop my practice.

I would also like to thank my drama teaching colleagues, in schools and universities, who share this wonderful vocation and continue to offer their craft, compassion and wisdom to ensure the young people in their care are blessed with the gift of theatre and empowered by the skills of drama.

I would also like to thank my family for their unwavering support – Michelle, Aidan, Lewis, Rhys and Max. A special thank you to Rhys for his artwork in preparing the diagrams for the chapters.

I would like also to acknowledge the support offered by the Rodney Seaborn Foundation in the preparation of this book and the great work they do to support playwriting in Australia.

PART ONE

Playwriting and young writers

1

Introduction

Why do people do art at school if they are not going to be an artist? Because it feeds other parts of ourselves and lets us think in different ways. ... Arts in high school give you another way of expressing yourself. Not just another way of telling a story it's another way of 'expressing' and some people will have a fluency in this form that they don't have in essay writing.

VANESSA BATES (PLAYWRIGHT)

What theatre does

An unexpected benefit of being a high school teacher was taking student leaders on experiential learning camps to develop their collaborative problem-solving skills. One of the most enjoyable activities was the high ropes course. This involved students, in a situation of high perceived risk and minimal actual risk, walking a tight-rope style obstacle course and pushing through feelings of fear. And, as long as they suspended their disbelief, the stakes were high.

The benefits of this learning experience were both dramatic and theatrical. Not only were students 'acting' in the role of protagonist struggling with their fears, they did so in front of an audience. Watching others face their fears was as 'educational' as completing it themselves. The students, as audience, saw how others coped with that new experience, and with that level of fear.

As a drama teacher, I realized that theatre provides students with a similar yet ultimately richer and more sophisticated learning experience. It also reminded me that theatre for and in schools should strive for the same level of urgency and liveness of a high ropes course. Students, as both actors and audience, thrive when engaging in a dramatic struggle and the spectacle of performance.

We know that the power of the theatre experience is found in its liveness. Theatre is real: a performance happens in front of an audience with living, breathing actors, in the same space and sharing the same air.

Yet, there is an understanding that this is *not real* – no one is really in danger or experiencing real misery or joy. Theatre provides an opportunity for students to live in these two worlds – the fictional and the real – providing a safe engagement with life's struggles, complications, joys and triumphs. Theatre asks an audience to engage with events and characters on the stage, challenging them to ask the following questions: What are they doing? How did they get there? What would I do in this situation? What if that was me?

It is this 'what if' of theatre that exercises students' empathetic muscles.

It asks audiences to consider questions they may have never considered before, about people whose lives they may never have imagined. It exposes an audience to extreme situations they would probably never have to experience. But it also asks them to reflect on events, like the death of a loved one or the betrayal of a friend, that they will almost certainly encounter. In this way, a play provides a rehearsal for the complexity of life.

We *learn* by watching characters experience extreme situations and emotions, carefully analysing their responses – like the ropes course – and imagine experiencing them ourselves.

The power of theatre and drama resides not only in the liveness – the visceral experience – but also in the intellectual questioning. A good play asks us to reflect on what it all means. Good theatre interrogates what it means to *be alive*. Ultimately, it is the ideas explored in the plays, through story, character or situation, that are the key to its lasting power.

As society progresses, or at least changes, the rituals of theatre are becoming more relevant and important. As young people's lives become increasingly mediated by digital identities and existences, the theatre's communal investigation of what it means to be human, in essence not just in appearance, is imperative. As Janet Neipris suggests, playwrights are asking 'How am I being?' rather than 'How am I looking?' (2005, p. 215).

As drama educators, our role is to demystify creative processes (Anderson, 2012). This is why encouraging young people to make theatre, to write a play, is so important. Not only should we develop a students' ability to understand and appreciate drama, we need to develop students' ability to manipulate and create it. When young people make or write theatre, the imaginative benefits of empathy and life rehearsal, so central to the audience experience, are amplified tenfold. Giving students the tools to create enables them to 'imagine' new worlds, to embody new characters and to develop new opinions and ideas, ideas perhaps previously unimaginable (Nicholson, 1998).

What a playwright does

The UK playwright Briony Lavery suggests that a playwright creates a vehicle – like a wheelwright, shipwright and other crafts that build things that carry other things. Playwrights manipulate humans and objects as conveyors of meaning and sites of meaning. A play is a vehicle for ideas. A playwright transforms ideas into moments, concepts into character and concerns into conflict – creating visual, aural and visceral experiences.

As I explore in the next two chapters, the writing process provides a range of benefits that go beyond those of the audience experience.

Writing a play offers a more concentrated and more invested experience of empathy and life rehearsal. Beyond observing the emotional journey of fictional characters, young playwrights construct them, imagining backgrounds and making life choices. In writing characters, playwrights explore what others believe and why they believe it, from within – by creating and taking on their perspectives and beliefs.

While in some ways a writer goes to the page to express what they believe, the writing process is also an act of construction. As Albee (2009) said, writing is an act of discovery. As a playwright, you are motivated to write a play to make sense of the chaos of your experiences of life. Drama is about questioning and challenging the assumptions of our lives (Sweet, 1993) reaching truth, not fact.

But rather than offering simple answers, a playwright imagines dramatic questions. Playwright and academic Steve Waters (2012) suggests that the playwright's role is to 'expose the sores of humanity, but not necessarily to cure them'.

And while a play will communicate something, there is also room for ambiguity and complexity. The more complex the questions, the less they respond to simple answers: audiences don't want to listen to a lecture. There will be opportunities in the play for the audience to engage with the ideas and formulate their own response.

In this way, a play is a dialogue. Audiences will make their own meaning from what they see and hear based on their life experiences and what they bring to the play.

What is a play?

A play is a text: a production is that text in a particular setting, with particular actors and scenery and lights and costumes, directed by a particular individual (Spencer, 2002, p. 291). A play text needs to understand the roles of director, designers and actors, and give them space to work. As the word play*wright* suggests, there is a more embodied component to the playwright than other writers. A playwright is writing a text and an (imagined) theatre experience that moves people, actors and characters, around in time and space, for spectators/ audience.

Yet, writing drama *is* a writerly skill, not fundamentally changed by the publication in two forms: text and production (Wandor, 2008, p. 4). Playwrights are writers; they create a story, its structure and journey, using the words and signs of dramatic language and the aural and visual symbols of the stage.

A playwright needs to create an 'affective space' (Taylor, 2002) – a simultaneous shared experience, employing sounds and sight to create text and image. And while all plays are written to be read first – by a literary manager or director – they are to be read as a text with unique qualities that demand a specific skill set to understand.

However, the Australian playwright Lachlan Philpott reminds us of the need to be wary of too limiting a definition of what a play *is*. Too strict an adherence to any one particular dramaturgy, especially one that privileges one particular view of what constitutes 'good playwriting' will stifle creativity:

> I would pick up work and [think] this is great, it's amazing – and [script assessors] were saying – yeah but it doesn't adhere to this, this and this dramaturgically – so it's not a good play – or it's not a play – you know that question … it's a very limiting question. 'But is it a play?' It's a very pompous question. Give the writer some respect – if they have imagined it [for] the stage, give it to a director who has a capacity to show initiative in a room with actors.

This book aims to provide a broad and open approach to playwriting, to embrace the range of definitions of a play and the variety of entry points for young writers.

My research

The book emanates from my research that explored the teaching and learning of playwriting in secondary schools in New South Wales, Australia. It focused on the experiences of students writing a short play for external assessment, in this case the NSW Higher School Certificate (HSC) Drama examination, and the pedagogical approaches adopted by the teachers.

I adopted a case study approach gathering data from teacher–student pairs in eight sites: nine teachers and eight Year 12 (final year) student playwrights in eight secondary schools. The participants were from both independent and government schools and were generally mid-career, with experience as both teachers and markers of the HSC. The students, while choosing to write a script for their individual projects, had limited prior experience of playwriting, with many never having written a play before commencing this project.

The qualitative data collected consisted of semi-structured interviews, play drafts, student logbooks, observations of teaching and learning sessions and workshop readings of the students' scripts.

My major finding was that there was, and is, a strong relationship between knowledge, creativity, agency and engagement. And that each of these components needs to be supported by scaffolded learning experiences that target playwriting and creativity specific skills and understanding.

What this book does

The purpose of this book is to encourage drama educators to introduce playwriting into their classroom, to give students the opportunity to not only engage with great theatre but to create it. It aims to support educators as they devise teaching and learning activities that will develop their students' skills and understanding of writing for the stage.

The aim of the text is to increase students' exposure to and proficiency in playwriting. It positions itself to complement the playbuilding and devising culture found in many of the theatre and drama curriculum documents and programmes across the Western drama education world. What I have found is that playwriting develops student agency and self efficacy in unique ways, offering benefits often overlooked in educational settings.

This text provides the resources and understanding for teachers to embark upon a program of playwriting with their students. It offers a new paradigm that will help make playwriting an enjoyable experience for teacher and student. It removes playwriting from either the too hard basket, the unknown or both. Through encouraging workshop collaboration, the paradigm also removes the perceived power hierarchy (a pyramid with a playwright at the top) that has seen drama educators retreat from playwriting in the classroom.

It recognizes that if we want to develop our writing culture, if we want to nurture and encourage young people to write for the stage, then we need to begin in high school (Hobgood, 1987). If we want to encourage a culture of storytelling and of empowering and embracing diverse voices and perspectives, then active engagement in a school setting will help even the playing field.

What this book doesn't do is assume or prescribe a formula. What can be learned are skills and understandings to empower students to create the play they imagine in the way that serves their idea. By developing student options through increased knowledge and skills, rather than offering an approach to write a play, this book aims to activate and generate creative confidence and creative capacity.

The image is about providing tools not limitations. As Gooch (2001) reminds us, 'There is no formula for writing plays. Each new play is a fresh challenge with its own special demands ... each idea implies a structure peculiar to itself' (p. 5). This book offers provocations and scaffolds rather than prescriptions. As Polly Stenham recalls, the best aspect of her playwriting education was that it 'demystified the process of writing for the stage'.

My intention is that this book will provide drama educators with the skills and confidence to teach playwriting in their classroom and workshops so students can access the benefits of this amazing creative activity and be equally empowered by understanding its processes.

References

Albee, E. (2009). 'Creativity Conversations'. In *Creativity Conversations*. Atlanta, GA: Emory University.

Anderson, M. (2012). *Masterclass in Drama Education: Transforming Teaching and Learning*. London: Continuum.

Gooch, S. (2001). *Writing a Play*. London: A & C Black.

Hobgood, B. M. (1987). 'The Mission of the Theatre Teacher'. *Journal of Aesthetic Education*, 21(1), 57–73.

Neipris, J. (2005). *To be a Playwright*. New York: Routledge.

Nicholson, H. (1998). 'Writing Plays: Taking Note of Genre'. In D. Hornbrook (Ed.), *On the Subject of Drama* (pp. 73–91). New York: Routledge.

Spencer, S. (2002). *The Playwright's Guidebook*. London: Faber and Faber.

Sweet, J. (1993). *The Dramatists Toolkit: The Craft of the Working Playwright*. Portsmouth, NH: Heinemann.

Taylor, V. (2002). *Stage Writing*. Ramsbury (England): Crowood Press.

Wandor, M. (2008). *The Art of Writing Drama*. London: Bloomsbury Academic.

Waters, S. (2012). *The Secret Life of Plays*. London: Nick Hern Books.

2

Why playwriting?

Introduction

*Well, rocks and trees and fairies and ... leotards – this
has nothing to do with real drama – drama is a real
man in a mess.*

DOROTHY HEATHCOTE (IN SMEDLEY, 1971)

*What we are ultimately doing is writing to find out
what we think about something.*

HILARY BELL

Drama, as Dorothy Heathcote suggested, is at its best when it
explores ideas and makes sense of experience. Because of that,
drama offers students opportunities to create and interpret
'human meaning through imagined action and language'
(Neelands, 1984, p. 6).

In this chapter, I will explore how playwriting offers unique
opportunities for students to develop their voice and foster a
sense of agency. I will show how writing a play engages young
people in an authentic process of self and critical reflection that is
essential to developing students' feelings of agency. It encourages

what Freire (1974, p. 4) called 'critical consciousness', enabling students to 'intervene in reality in order to change it'.

I will also explore how increasing students' playwriting proficiency maximizes these benefits, perhaps turning a one-off learning *experience* into a long-term proficiency.

What is agency?

Agency is a belief in our ability to influence our environment. An individual with agency has 'the power to shape their life circumstances and the course of their lives' (Bandura, 2006, p. 164).

Playwriting offers a level of personal autonomy not found in other aspects of drama courses that are often focused on group devised work. Writing a play involves a process and a product; independent self-reflection and commitment to an idea that culminates in a written artefact. This 'text', read and performed by others, gives playwriting a gravitas often not present in other aspects of a drama workshop. And this personal autonomy bolsters personal investment.

Playwriting focuses students on finding a 'burning' issue in their world, one that *needs* to be addressed. This encourages 'cultural citizenship' – a willingness and ability to understand and critique social life (Stevenson, 1997). As Albee suggests, we write a play because we wish to influence thought, to reflect society back on to itself, to challenge prevailing ideas and practices (Albee in Flanagan, 1996). The decision to write a play originates in a specific desire to communicate, to engage in a social dialogue with an audience: you choose a topic that is a pressing issue for you that you want to bring to the attention of an audience (Taylor, 2002, p. 14).

Playwriting encourages on imaginative and symbolic thinking. The creation of worlds inhabited by characters of their imagination, who 'reflect ... and make corrective judgements' (Bandura, 2006), contribute to playwriting's significant and unique potential to develop student agency. Symbolic thinking is essential to agency: It creates the power to visualize futures, and to 'construct, evaluate and modify alternative courses of action' (Bandura, 2006, p. 164). It develops students' abilities to reimagine their world in a way that challenges its injustices or exposes its inconsistencies. It is this creative dimension that makes us human (Freire, 1974).

The self-knowledge and reflection encouraged by playwriting offers students a profound opportunity to reflect on their world and their place in it. By encouraging students to consider other perspectives (Fisher, 2008), playwriting has the potential to develop their sense of empathy (Jester and Stoneman, 2012). As playwright and teacher Lachlan Philpot suggests:

> It's about making them aware of their own personal politics – including, but more than, their world view – making them aware that they come from a particular background and that they have been brought up in a particular way and they have made assumptions about a lot of privileges that they have had – so you are developing [their] sense of where they are placed in the world.

Through critical and creative self-reflection, a playwright imagines a vision for their play that reflects their 'thoughts, intuitions, and attitudes' (Smiley, 2005, p. 18). Playwriting is fundamentally personal as 'the idea for the play comes from within you ... your values and attitudes, ... your hopes, fears and desires' (Taylor, 2002, p. 27). As it inspires students to mine their life experiences to explore significant issues, student playwrights often choose ideas that are closely linked to their own life dilemmas.

The personal nature of their ideas means that the playwriting process involves a level of risk and vulnerability. Playwriting entails self-exposure. A play catapults a playwright's 'opinions, ideas, passions and prejudices into the forum for debate' (Taylor, 2002, p. 27). It opens their innermost thoughts to audience scrutiny – their aesthetic, philosophical, social and personal identity. But it is precisely the willingness to take on that risk, to engage in the social dialogue and to stand by their ideas, that makes playwriting so rich and beneficial to student agency. As Sklar (2008) indicates:

> When children write plays, their wishes, fears and secrets face an audience. An audience isn't a do-gooder making nice. It is an authority figure with a grudge against one's race or class. When it laughs at the jokes or applauds, it can be trusted. It is saying this play – and by extension its author – fits into the world on its own merits. In effect, each playwright declares, 'This is who I am. I count.' The audience, in its turn, validates this assessment. (p. 136)

To increase the impact of their theatre and diminish their potential vulnerability, playwrights adopt a universal metaphor or vehicle to create artistic distance. They create a theatrical representation of these human dilemmas: their attempts to make sense of their world, their desire to question society and/ or explore a deeply felt issue. Through this use of metaphor, writing a play is an opportunity to act – to affect change through raising questions and sharing observations.

By engaging with universal concerns beyond themselves, playwrights contribute to the cultural dialogue. The creation of an artefact (the play) and the event (production) do more than just comment or reflect the playwright's social context – it becomes part of it. A play written by students does not just reflect community values; when read or performed by others it becomes a part of that community and is a critical interaction with that culture (Doyle, 1993). Doyle argues, 'We miss much of the potential for drama if we do not realise that it can play a part in reformulating culture just as it does in objectifying it' (p. 68). Young people use the arts to 'transform' their understanding of the world and to make symbolic meaning of their lives (Mooney, 2005). Through the social aspect of a play, in workshop and performance (real or imagined), students participate in the cultural dialogue. This opportunity for self-expression may be otherwise absent in their world. Gattenhof (2006, p. 30) argues that 'to have their voices heard in response to issues that impact upon them ... creates a sense of belonging for young people whose voice is often marginalised in society'. Drama and theatre thus empower students to transform society.

Playwriting as learning

As we have seen, writing a play is a reflective process that improves self-awareness. However, the playwriting experience provides opportunities for students to do more than just restate or express their views. While it clarifies and makes them more conscious of their current positions, it also leads to students *generating* new ideas and opinions. The personal nature of much playwriting means that students *work through* the issues they are experiencing, turning the rehearsal nature of theatre into a laboratory of thought, offering possibilities and opportunities for aesthetic and personal growth. In my research, the students considered playwriting as an opportunity to express their views on 'big' issues that had particular relevance to their lives. They approached playwriting as an opportunity to question aspects of society and to make sense of the world around them, and to work through key autobiographical concerns. The desire to change society was evident in all the plays, demonstrating the capacity of theatre to empower: to build our future, instead of just waiting for it (Boal, 1992, p. 16).

However, what emerged in my research was the relationship between the students' ability to *realize* the feelings of agency intrinsic in the process and their ability to manipulate the conventions and stylistic features of the play form. As their ideas became more complex and sophisticated – often because of the empathy required in character creation – the students rethought simplistic theatrical solutions. As a result, their plays became less didactic and more 'questioning' – open rather than closed.

Empathy changes students' views on what a play should and could do. This learning encourages students to create more sophisticated vehicles or metaphors, focusing on emotional rather than rational engagement. Students learn that emotional truth is the way to create meaningful, affective theatre. Learning about playwriting and learning about human behaviour coexist.

Agency and proficiency

Plays need to not only be interesting for the playwright, but connect with and affect an audience of others (Edgar, 2009). Student agency is increased and broadened by developing playwriting proficiency. *Learning how* to write about the world allows us to rewrite it – to critically read and then to transform it (Freire and Macedo, 1987, p. 35). *Learning how* to understand and manipulate the signs and symbols that constitute stage language (Elam, 1980; Pfister, 1988) gives students new modes of expression and the opportunity for thought previously 'inconceivable' (Nicholson, 1998, p. 79). Nicholson suggests that 'as students take control of the dramatic form [they understand how to] construct dramatic texts as vehicles of thought and communication' (1998, p. 84). Increased proficiency, and increased skill in the language of the stage, allows students to not only express their existing ideas and concerns, but develop new ideas and social and cultural skills.

Playwriting with students is often approached as a beneficial experience: a chance to voice their ideas rather than an opportunity for rigorous craft development. Yet building proficiency encourages students to feel justified in offering their play to an audience. They feel entitled to contribute their views, believing, rightly, that their perspective is valuable, and their work is good.

Understandably, students' perceptions of their playwriting proficiency impact their agency and feelings of self-efficacy. Playwriting helps students understand the story they are living and to share their realizations. Writing a play empowers students by validating their experiences *and their interpretation* of those experiences. It offers students the opportunity to see their ideas and life experiences as valid content for a play (Sklar, 2008), elevating them from the ordinary to the (potentially) universal.

Why teach playwriting?

The ability to realize their objectives and write a piece of effective and affecting theatre is impacted by students' control of the craft. A belief in intrinsic creativity may well suggest that a play is already 'in' the student and only needs to be 'released', but this idea is not supported by my research. Teaching and learning activities need to support the students' actual, and perceived, skill development. For playwriting to encourage agency and empathy, the writing process needs to scaffold learning experiences to ensure opportunity is accompanied by skill development.

Agency is more than freedom to *choose* ideas; students need the proficiency to articulate them. Students need proficiency in theatrical literacy and dramatic vocabulary in order to 'imagine' new opinions and ideas and to imagine new ways to express them. Understanding theatrical language enables students to develop a sophisticated metaphor for their autobiographical experiences and observations. Freedom is real if students have the words to express their views and the clarity of thinking to formulate new ones. To rewrite the world, one needs the literacy to write and the vocabulary to 'rethink' it (Freire and Macedo, 1987). Playwriting knowledge does not restrain, it enables, and to remove or withhold it is an act with strong implications for agency.

Conclusion

Students not only benefit from the opportunity to 'experience' playwriting but also need to engage with teaching and learning activities to scaffold and develop playwriting knowledge and skill. My research suggests greater emphasis on playwriting, both in teacher education and classroom practice, will increase teacher and student engagement with this valuable process.

This chapter explored the multiple benefits for agency and self-awareness offered by the playwriting process. A play provides a metaphorical, and thus relatively safe, discussion of 'big' ideas and concerns in the lives of young people. The autobiographical nature of plays, and successfully navigating the risk involved, reinforces the students' sense of agency. It encourages them to reflect on their life stories and, through metaphor, find universal observations and ideas to communicate their opinions and interrogate the world in which they live. Similarly, a lack of playwriting proficiency limits students' ability to realize their potential, with significant negative impact on students' feelings of self-efficacy and agency.

Developing greater playwriting proficiency in our young people, and in our schools, will work to broaden the skill base of young writers, and in turn work towards encouraging diversity and democracy of voices, in content and in form. The re-igniting of interest in this under-researched and under-utilized creative process has the potential to offer authentic opportunities for students to grapple with 'big' ideas and develop a lasting proficiency that fosters symbolic and creative thinking. Playwriting encourages students to develop their reflective skills and increase self-knowledge, while also fostering a belief in their ability to contribute to and influence their world.

At a time when the need for greater understanding of ourselves and of each other is so pressing (Anderson, 2014), increased engagement with playwriting and its ability to encourage both empathy and personal growth seems a practice that deserves much greater attention. The habits of mind and skills of agency, such as critical reflection and creative invention, are essential skills for our young people to possess. The playwriting process, involving workshops and performances, also encourages 'actual' collaboration and community engagement in a time when contact with others is becoming increasingly virtual and mediated.

The benefits of playwriting to our students are many and varied, in both the short and long term. It has the potential to generate more diverse and vibrant voices, as well as to encourage more engaged and culturally aware citizens who positively contribute to a more empathetic and vigorously democratic society. The full range and extent of these benefits are yet to be fully realized and a paradigm shift in the classroom is needed if we are to see students gain greater access. Extending opportunities for students to exercise this voice is beneficial to all involved, ensuring an enriched and diverse critical and cultural conversation.

Summary

- Playwriting offers unique opportunities to encourage and develop students' feelings of agency.
- The process of writing a play encourages students to explore, develop and generate their views of the world.
- Writing a play is a valuable experience with the benefits of empathy and agency heightened by greater proficiency.
- This proficiency can and should be developed with scaffolded teaching and learning activities.
- Greater playwriting proficiency in young people will work to develop their opportunities to have their voice heard which will hopefully lead to a diversity and democracy of voices on our stages.

References

Anderson, M. (2014). 'The Challenge of Post-normality to Drama Education and Applied Theatre'. *Research in Drama Education: The Journal of Applied Theatre and Performance*, 19(1), 110–20.

Bandura, A. (2006). 'Toward a Psychology of Human Agency'. *Perspectives on Psychological Science*, 1(2), 164–80.

Boal, A. (1992). *Games for Actors and Non-Actors* (Trans. A. Jackson, second ed.). London and New York: Routledge.

Doyle, C. (1993). *Raising Curtains on Education: Drama as a Site for Critical Pedagogy*. Wesport, CT: Bergin and Garvey.

Edgar, D. (2009). *How Plays Work*. London: Nick Hearn Books.

Elam, K. (1980). *The Semiotics of Theatre and Drama*. London and New York: Methuen.

Fisher, M. (2008). 'Catching Butterflies'. *English Education*, 40(2), 94–100.

Flanagan, W. (1996). 'Edward Albee, The Art of Theatre No. 4'. *The Paris Review* (39). Retrieved from http://www.theparisreview.org/interviews/4350/the-art-of-theater-no-4-edward-albee

Freire, P. (1974). *Education for Critical Consciousness*. London: Sheed & Ward.

Freire, P. and Macedo, D. (1987). *Literacy: Reading the Word and the World*. London: Routledge and Kegan Paul.

Gattenhof, S. (2006). *Drivers of Change: Contemporary Australian Theatre for Young People*. City East, QLD: Drama Australia.

Jester, C. and Stoneman, C. (2012). *Playwriting Across the Curriculum*. London and New York: Routledge.

Mooney, M. (2005). 'Morphing into New Spaces: Transcoding Drama'. *NJ*, 29(1), 25–35.

Neelands, J. (1984). *Making Sense of Drama: A Guide to Classroom Practice*. London: Heinemann Educational Books.

Nicholson, H. (1998). 'Writing Plays: Taking Note of Genre'. In D. Hornbrook (Ed.), *On the Subject of Drama* (pp. 73–91). New York: Routledge.

Pfister, M. (1988). *The Theory and Analysis of Drama*. Cambridge: Cambridge University Press.

Sklar, D. J. (2008). 'Playmaking'. *Teaching Artist Journal*, 6(2), 135–45.

Smedley, R. (1971). 'Three Looms Waiting'. Mantle of the expert. com.

Smiley, S. (2005). *Playwriting: The Structure of Action*. New Haven and London: Yale University Press.

Stevenson, N. (1997). 'Globalization, National Cultures and Cultural Citizenship'. *The Sociological Quarterly*, 38(1), 41–66.

Taylor, V. (2002). *Stage Writing*. Ramsbury (England): Crowood Press.

3

Creativity and engagement

You've got to maintain the innocence of a child playing in a garden, making stuff up ...

POLLY STENHAM

Introduction

One of the important findings that emerged from my research was how much impact the teachers' and students' views of creativity had on the teaching and learning strategies they programmed for the playwriting classroom. In my research, there was a belief that playwriting was a particularly creative activity, but that teachers needed to be careful and reserved in their interventions so as not to taint the students' natural or naive creative ideas.

I call this belief the *myth of intrinsic creativity*: that creativity is a special talent *within* some students, and not in others, and that creativity needs to be released rather than developed or taught.

This popular understanding of creativity is further distorted by the idealist and Romantic view that creative people are special and/or 'geniuses' and that creativity is an innate gift (Weisberg, 1993). This perspective seems to encourage a non-interventiontist approach to teaching and learning, thinking that the teacher is largely powerless in the face of mystical creativity and only needs to work out who the creative students are and to 'give them room to work' (Boden, 2004, p. 15). In this school of thought, teaching and learning strategies are corrupting rather than enabling. Popular Romantic idealist assumptions perpetuate the focus on the individual and innate nature of creativity. The problem with a belief that creativity is unknowable and mysterious is that it encourages the view that it cannot be analysed, developed or taught.

This chapter argues that these approaches are based on an obsolete view of creativity and creative processes, and on contestable views of the relationship between knowledge and imagination which are detrimental to students' creative capacity.

Can playwriting be taught?

The tension between creative practice and pedagogy has a long history. Playwrights in particular often express the conviction that playwriting really cannot be taught (Albee, 2009). Many texts on playwriting pedagogy expressed a suspicion of 'teaching the craft' (see, for example, Archer, 1960; Ayckbourn, 2002; Napoleon, 2010; Selden, 1946). A number of playwrights and theorists argue that 'lessons' in the playwright's craft are, at best, counterproductive and, at worst, damaging to the authenticity of the young playwright's voice (see Herrington and Brian, 2006; Napoleon, 2010; Norden, 2007). American playwright Jose Rivera argues that a teacher cannot improve or generate *talent* (Herrington and Brian, 2006, p. viii), and Henry Hwang suggests that you are either a playwright or you are not (p. viii). Some playwrights argue that teaching playwriting is counterproductive, and that it diminishes the potential and uniqueness of the emerging playwright (Herrington and Brian, 2006). The belief is that creative writing courses 'damage a distinctive talent' (Norden,

2007, p. 646) and stifle creative promise (Herrington and Brian, 2006, p. vii). There is a fear that teaching imposes rules that repress the individuality and creativity of each playwright, and that it interferes with intrinsic talent. The playwrights' attitude seems to be that to gain mastery of their craft, there is a body of knowledge that can and should be *learnt* – it just should not and cannot be *taught*. Herrington and Brian's (2006) question 'Is there a danger that the very act of instruction can, in fact, stifle the creative promise?' (p. viii) reflects a belief that pedagogy corrupts rather than edifies.

The relationship between 'talent', 'creativity' and 'pedagogy' is at the heart of this discussion.

This seems to be related, as observed by the teachers in my study, to a belief in the mystical nature of inspiration. Waters (2013) suggests that some playwrights believe that the writing process is 'unknowable' and can really only be understood in a visceral rather than a cerebral way (Waters, 2013, p. 137). He argues that they fear that thinking too much about it, looking too closely at the secrets, may scare off creativity (Waters, 2013, p. 139). Albee (2009) supported this mystifying of the creative process when he argued that creativity is not something he understands and that he was not sure it could even be discussed. Fountain (2007) encapsulates this position by suggesting 'the magical alchemy which creates great theatre is not conjured up by following a rulebook' (p. 113).

My research suggests this suspicion of instruction is alive and well in the classroom. What surprised me the most, and is reinforced by my continued work with teachers, was that the students' and teachers' views of creativity were at the core of the pedagogical dynamic. Initially, the focus of my research was to investigate the influence of dramaturgical theory on teaching and learning activities and, subsequently, on the kind and quality of student plays. However, it emerged in my study that the teachers and students did not *explicitly* engage with semiotic or genre theory, and (generally speaking) there was very little structured teaching at all.

While the teachers and students acknowledged this lack of theoretical or pedagogical input, it was often explained as a virtue not an omission. Teachers indicated they did not follow a 'program' but carried out student–teacher sessions based on point-of-need discussions with the individual student. The teachers reported that they did not consult playwriting texts in preparing for their interactions, believing their role was to respond as an experienced theatre goer once there was something to critique. In practice, that meant 'go away and write something and I will tell you if it is any good'.

Their view of creativity, and what can be done to assist the creative process, defined the teaching and learning practices and, in turn, the students' experience. The desire not to intervene in the creative process was based on their belief that a structured course was unnecessary and unhelpful. The teachers' distrust of teaching and learning intervention was connected to their view that the student's unique talent, their creativity and individual voice, needed to be protected from the limiting effect of rules and knowledge and not wanting to impose a 'house style' on their students. Some of the participants even indicated a belief in innate creative talent that did not need domain knowledge.

I found that creativity in the classroom was heavily influenced by often un-examined myths that creativity cannot be taught and therefore playwriting cannot be taught.

Yet, as Edgar (2009) argues, there is an inconsistency in the views on 'training' in the theatre arts, in that actors and designers and others are encouraged to acquire their skills formally, while writers (and directors) 'are supposed to acquire their skills telepathically' (p. xii).

In this chapter, I will present an approach to teaching that is influenced by a view of creativity that rejects assumptions of innate individual 'specialness' and understands it as a social and collaborative activity. I propose that adopting a 'systems' view of creativity (Csikszentmihalyi, 2008) could have a significant positive impact on the way we teach playwriting in the classroom.

What is creativity?

While there are many definitions of creativity, I suggest that, in contrast to the idealist view, creativity is both an ability and a process. Creativity generates products (ideas and artefacts) that are both novel and appropriate, of high quality (Sternberg, Kaufman and Pretz, 2002) and/or significant to a field (Bailin, 1988, p. 4). Creativity is a capacity to generate 'ideas and artefacts that are new, surprising and valuable' (Boden, 2004, p. 1). It is a potential present in everyone, not just the gifted few, and with the right training and knowledge can be developed (Haseman, 2012, p. 41).

The core of creativity is possibility thinking – 'a shift from what is to what might be' (Craft et al., 2013, p. 539) achieved through imagination, questioning and play (Craft, 2000, p. 7). The emphasis on play and finding possibilities is the core of creative collaboration in the classroom.

Rather than a flash of inspiration followed by creative execution, creativity is a recursive process (Csikszentmihalyi, 1996, p. 83) requiring discipline, perseverance, evaluation and *frequent* moments of insight (Sawyer, 2012, p. 116). For Sawyer, the stages of the creative process are iterative and overlapping (2012, p. 138). Craft (2005, p. 6) argues that creativity involves two types of thinking – imaginative-generative and critical-evaluative – reminding us that 'critical judgement is central to creativity' (Bailin, 2011, p. 212).

Knowing how to approach student creativity in the classroom can be helped by embracing the idea that creativity occurs in many ways, on several levels. For example, creativity exists as both *Big-C* creativity, such as the writing of an award-winning play, novel or poem, and *little-c* creativity, such as discoveries and contributions that are personally significant and/or new for the individual or group (Berghetto and Kaufman, 2007). In the context of playwriting pedagogy, writing a play personally significant to the student (little-c) is the product of the same type of thinking that results in the *Big-C* Pulitzer Prize-winning play. All Big-C creative accomplishments begin as *little-c* creativity. If we see creative ideas as resulting from everyday thinking, enriched by skills, motivation and knowledge (Weisberg, 1993), then the mysticism surrounding the writing process (including writer's block) is removed.

Creativity as improvisation

Learning is 'a creative improvisational process' (Sawyer, 2010, p. 184) and the ability to experiment with and exchange ideas in collaboration enables creativity (and creativity skills) to be *constructed* (rather than discovered or unleashed). Vygotsky called creativity 'combinatorial' – suggesting that the brain 'combines and creatively reworks elements of ... past experience and uses them to create new propositions and new behaviour' (Vygotsky, 2004, p. 9).

The importance of improvisation for creativity is often overlooked by definitions that focus on novelty and innovation (Ingold and Hallam, 2007). Ingold and Hallam argue that significant creativity is required, for instance, in the maintenance of a tradition and the replication of an art form (2007, p. 5). For students working on a play, the quality of creativity required in producing this complex art form and the improvisation needed to respond to the emerging challenges are more important measures of creativity than an assessment of the novelty of the final product. Further, improvisation occurs within a body of knowledge and a context – of others, of ideas, of culture (Ingold and Hallam, 2007, p. 6). This also underlines the importance of collaboration to creativity; that we collaborate with others, and with the ideas of others, throughout the creative process. We improvise within a given framework – a domain. The creativity of our improvisations, the value of our knowledge and our manipulation of the forms within these parameters are assessed by a field or gatekeepers (Sawyer, 2012, p. 348), including classroom teachers for student playwrights and literary managers for professionals.

The systems view of creativity

The systems approach to creativity explores the importance of knowledge for creative thinking and the cycles of imaginative and analytical thinking. For Csikszentmihalyi, creativity occurs in 'a system composed of three elements: a culture that contains symbolic rules, a person[1] who brings novelty into the symbolic domain, and a field of experts (or gatekeepers) who recognize and validate the innovation' (1996, p. 6). In the systems view, creativity is 'an act, ideal, or product that changes an existing domain, or that transforms an existing domain into a new one' (Csikszentmihalyi, 1996, p. 28). Thus, to be creative you need to know about the area in which you want to contribute – to add to new ideas and combine existing ones in new ways.

To assess the work for originality and value, and whether the work adds to a domain (culture) and will be accepted by the field, the creative individual(s) will need knowledge, skill and understanding of the gatekeepers' rules and/or expectations.

While this may appear too clinical, think of the fate of musicians courting record companies or of playwrights sending scripts to literary managers and novelists sending manuscripts to publishers. Knowledge of what is 'out there' is necessary to know how to *add* to the culture. The creative playwright will internalize domain knowledge in order to contribute ideas that will be accepted by members of the field (Csikszentmihalyi, 1999).

Creativity and knowledge

As Burton (2001, p. 115) argues, drama is symbolic: 'Every word that is spoken has been chosen for the message it conveys; the set and every object on it is important to the play; and everything about the play is significant'. Playwrights manipulate the

---

[1]In my analysis 'person' can represent an individual or a partnership/group that offers up a creative product.

elements of drama and use theatre semiotics, with its signs and common language, to create metaphor and communicate to an audience (Aston and Savona, 1991; Elam, 1980). The playwriting student therefore needs 'dramatic literacy', an ability to 'speak' the language of the stage and its 'verbal, ... visual and acoustic codes' (Pfister, 1988). Learning to understand and manipulate 'imaginative shorthand' (Smiley, 2005, p. 160), the signs and symbols that constitute stage language, and knowledge of the unique qualities of the play text with its multiple simultaneous signs (Hayman, 1977), will equip students with the 'tools' of creation (Jefferson and Anderson, 2009).

Knowledge of playwriting conventions, rather than stifling or contaminating creativity, is a pre-requisite for generating something new. It is only through understanding how existing techniques meet and/or no longer suit their artistic goals are young people (or any writer) able to develop control, play within existing forms and generate new ideas. As Bailin (2011, p. 211) argues, 'It is an understanding of the rules and conventions, of the reasons for them, and of what is at issue in complying with them, which enables an artist to know when to violate these rules'.

And, importantly, this knowledge is not innate. Aesthetic understanding (Anderson, 2012) – the knowledge of the unique qualities of the play text with its creation of multiple, simultaneous sources of meaning (Hayman, 1977) – is necessary to enable students to develop aesthetic control (Anderson and Jefferson, 2009) and create their own work. As Hatcher (1996) argues, 'The wise playwright learns not from narrow specifics ... but from wide generalities' (p. 207). Providing access to the breadth of techniques and conventions empowers the students, offering options rather than limitations.

To create opportunities for students to gain these tools for thought and expression (Nicholson, 1998), the playwriting teacher will encourage students to develop an understanding of the meanings of these codes, signs and symbols. To understand genre and styles, students need opportunities to experiment with creating, recreating and subverting them, and to see *how* meaning is made on stage and through text. As Burton (2001) argues, the ability to create effective drama texts 'depends on our ability to use and understand symbol' (p. 114).

The approach to pedagogy encouraged by this book creates teaching and learning activities that develop students' knowledge and skills in both creative processes and playwriting semiotics. Activities that deconstruct how meaning is made on the stage (understanding) are supplemented with opportunities for students to develop and realize those skills (control). Much like a musician learning various styles and modes and then composing new music informed by all they have learnt, this approach assumes that what we write is informed by what we know – and that this knowledge needs to be deconstructed, activated and mobilized. Knowledge will not only enable the playwright to learn the conventions, but awareness of a spectrum of genres, techniques and conventions, past and present, informs and enables the creation of the new (Esslin, 1965).

Writing of a play has always required knowledge of past practices (Gombrich, 1966; Hardy, 1993; Waters, 2012) and innovative works reimagine existing conventions (Castagno, 2001; Esslin, 1965). The pedagogical approach outlined in this book also encourages thinking explicitly about creativity (Lassig, 2013) to develop students' awareness of their own creative processes. Thinking metacognitively about creativity encourages students to experiment with approaches and self-assess their creative experiences (Lassig, 2013, p. 11). Understanding their creative strengths and preferences can increase their skill at completing challenging creative tasks.

Flow as a lens to understand engagement

A semiotic approach to playwriting pedagogy, understanding the link between aesthetic control and creativity, has a positive effect on engagement. If students approach a creative task with insufficient skill or knowledge, they are likely to become frustrated and disengage (Starko, 2005).

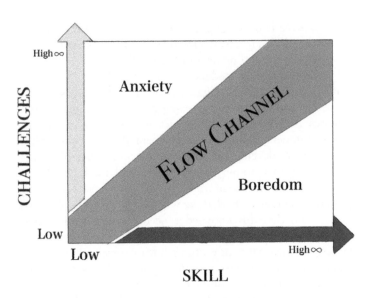

FIGURE 3.1 *The flow channel (adapted from Csikszentmihalyi, 2008, p. 74).*

As Csikszentmihalyi (2014) argues, a key challenge for education is attending to problems with student engagement; the 'affective, emotional, motivational' (p. 130) aspects of learning. The belief in intrinsic creativity, viewing it as an individual gift or talent, means that problems with creative expression are problems with, or for, the individual. An inability to remain engaged is therefore a problem with an individual's application or innate talent. If a student reaches an impasse, then perhaps they do not have 'it'. To encourage a belief in intrinsic creativity, and downplay the importance of domain knowledge, could do as much to extinguish the spark of creativity as over-prescriptive instruction and direction.

The systems model explores the relationship between creativity, engagement and knowledge. Csikszentmihalyi (2008) explains that an individual experiences high levels of engagement, what he calls 'flow', when the challenge of a particular task is met with a corresponding skill level.

Flow is a state of heightened awareness, characterized by deep concentration, a focus on a clear goal, a diminishing awareness of time passing and a sense of control. Activities that generate flow are so gratifying that the task becomes intrinsically motivating (Csikszentmihalyi, 1993, p. 39; Csikszentmihalyi, 2008; Csikszentmihalyi, Rathunde and Whalen, 1993, p. 15), 'autotelic, that it is worth doing for its own sake' (Csikszentmihalyi, Rathunde and Whalen, 1993, p. 15) and encourage repetition (Csikszentmihalyi, 1993, p. 39).

To remain in flow, there needs to be an optimal match between skill and challenge: If the task is too easy, the student becomes bored; if the task is too difficult, the student is paralysed or anxious. This dynamic process pushes people to higher levels of performance (Csikszentmihalyi, 2008), as 'flow' encourages students to increase their skill development to increase engagement. That is, students will embrace new challenges to avoid boredom and pursue new skills and knowledge to avoid anxiety (Csikszentmihalyi, Rathunde and Whalen, 1993, p. 15). While describing moments of extraordinary focus, linking motivation and skill in the concept of flow can help us understand more common and longer-term experiences of productive engagement.

Flow is particularly valuable for our understanding of self-directed learning in all students, not only those working on a play. For a student to engage, and then maintain that engagement in a creative and challenging task, the skill level must continue to grow to match the increasing challenge. The idea of flow also challenges the belief that creativity is best fostered by a non-interventionist pedagogical approach. The systems theory, and flow in particular, suggests that neither engagement nor creativity is innate, and that active pedagogy is needed to develop and maintain both.

This has implications for teaching playwriting and teaching for and about creativity. If we think of creativity as an innate ability, then naive talent is 'noble' and should be kept free from the corrupting influence of teaching. As I have suggested (and will discuss further), the teaching and learning a teacher plans for their students is a product of their view of creativity. Thus, a non-interventionist approach would see an absence of structured teaching and a lack of theoretical or pedagogical input as best practice. However, this ambivalence towards the teaching of playwriting coexisted with a belief that playwriting was difficult.

Csikszentmihalyi's (2008) concept of flow, and the conditions associated with its occurrence, challenges this idealist belief in intrinsic creativity and provides evidence for the value of teaching and skill acquisition in creative tasks. Rather than allowing students 'room to work', teaching and learning strategies based on a belief that creativity is an intrinsic gift can act to diminish the students' ability to meet the increasing challenge of the task and reinforces the idea that some students are just not creative. As 'flow' theory predicts, this non-interventionist approach adversely affects student's motivation and continued engagement, resulting in paralysis and cynicism (Csikszentmihalyi, 2008) which in turn creates further challenges to engagement.

And if creativity is innate, a student's inability to 'create' is defined as a product of a lack of application, rather than a lack of skill, and will result in pedagogy that imposes more stringent deadlines and encourages students to 'work harder'. According to 'flow' theory, disengagement originates in, or is exacerbated by, a skill deficit and a feeling that a challenge is too great. Thus 'cracking the whip' will not address the core issue. Csikszentmihalyi (2008) argued that achievement and proficiency are key to intrinsic motivation, and that there is a relationship between complexity and flow (1993).

The belief in intrinsic creativity makes teachers unnecessarily disengaged from the creative aspect of playwriting, and unaware of the importance of ongoing creative teaching and learning throughout the process. This book has emerged from a passionate belief that knowledge, skill development and awareness of creative processes are enabling rather than prescriptive. Increased playwriting literacy enables and empowers the student, making them less reliant on the teacher and more able to assess their own work and reach their creative promise.

Conclusion

When teaching creativity to students at university, I use the example of Michelangelo to explain the importance of knowledge and skill in realizing creative potential. The Pieta in Rome is a remarkable piece of sculpture, perhaps my favourite piece of art. The mythology around Michelangelo was that he believed he could see the art inside the marble and that all he was doing was 'releasing it'. The important unspoken part of that myth is the skill with hammer and chisel necessary to work with marble and to produce such lifelike creations – even if they do appear to him as visions. The precision and practical dexterity, as well as knowledge of how marble reacts under different kinds of force, is perhaps his real mythological feat.

Rethinking the teacher's role in managing creativity needs to begin with a challenge to our assumptions about what creativity is – and to abandon the belief in intrinsic creativity that understates the role of knowledge and skill development. The 'flow' theory provides an effective lens to examine creative processes. Skill (and knowledge) development impacts intrinsic motivation. Further, the insights are significant for teaching for, with and about creativity. It is not only students who will benefit from an awareness of the need to increase skills to meet increasingly difficult challenges. Teacher professional learning that specifically addresses creativity will increase teacher efficacy, confidence and, ultimately, enjoyment in teaching and managing creative tasks.

Summary

- Myth of intrinsic creativity, and the associated non-interventionist pedagogical approach, negatively impacts the student's ability to succeed in the creative task of playwriting.
- Playwriting, including the ability to generate creative ideas and creatively solve problems, can be taught.

- Creativity is a capacity and a process. The core of creativity is possibility thinking in the context of play, risk taking and collaboration.
- Creativity can be expressed in a range of ways. It can be found in a process of replicating a form incorporating authentic perspectives, or it can be a product that is new, surprising and valuable.
- Creativity occurs as a collaboration with others and with ideas in a system. Knowledge of the domain improves students' ability to be creative in that domain.
- Csikszentmihalyi's idea of flow helps us understand how to keep our students engaged in the difficult challenge of writing a play.
- Engagement and creativity are both improved through increased knowledge and proficiency.

References

Albee, E. (2009). 'Creativity Conversations'. In *Creativity Conversations*. Atlanta, Georgia: Emory University.

Anderson, M. (2012). *Masterclass in Drama Education: Transforming Teaching and Learning*. London: Continuum.

Anderson, M. and Jefferson, M. (2009). *Teaching the Screen: Film Education for Generation Next*. Sydney: Allen and Unwin.

Archer, W. (1960). *Playmaking: A Manual of Craftmanship*. New York: Dover Publications, Inc.

Aston, E. and Savona, G. (1991). *Theatre as Sign System: A Semiotics of Text and Performance*. London and New York: Routledge.

Ayckbourn, A. (2002). *The Crafty Art of Playmaking*. London: Faber and Faber.

Bailin, S. (1988). *Achieving Extraordinary Ends: An Essay on Creativity*. Dordrecht, Boston and Lancaster: Kluwer Academic Publishers.

Bailin, S. (2011). 'Creativity and Drama Education'. In S. Schonmann (Ed.), *Key Concepts in Theatre/Drama Education* (pp. 209–13). Rotterdam: Sense Publications.

Berghetto, R. A. and Kaufman, J. C. (2007). 'The Genesis of Creative Greatness: Mini-c and the Expert Performance Approach'. *High Ability Studies*, 18(1), 59–61.

Boden, M. (2004). *The Creative Mind: Myths and Mechanisms*. New York: Routledge.

Burton, B. (2001). *Living Drama*. Sydney, Melbourne, Brisbane, Perth: Longman.

Castagno, P. (2001). *New Playwriting Strategies: A Language-Based Approach to Playwriting*. New York: Routledge.

Craft, A. (2000). *Creativity Across the Primary Curriculum: Framing and Developing Practice*. London and New York: Routledge.

Craft, A. (2005). *Creativity in Schools: Tensions and Dilemmas*. London: Routledge.

Craft, A., Cremin, T., Burnard, P., Dragovic, T. and Chappell, K. (2013). 'Possibility Thinking: Culminative Studies of an Evidence-Based Concept of Creativity?' *Education*, 3(13), 538–56.

Csikszentmihalyi, M. (1993). 'Activity and Happiness: Toward a Science of Occupation'. *Occupational Science: Australia*, 1(1), 38–42.

Csikszentmihalyi, M. (1996). *Creativity: Flow and the Psychology of Discovery and Invention*. New York: Harper Collins.

Csikszentmihalyi, M. (1999). 'Implications of a Systems Perspective for the Study of Creativity'. In R. J. Sternberg (Ed.), *Handbook of Creativity* (pp. 313–35). Cambridge: Cambridge University Press.

Csikszentmihalyi, M. (2008). *Flow: The Psychology of Optimal Experience*. New York: Harper Perennial Modern Classics.

Csikszentmihalyi, M. (2014). 'Flow in Education'. In M. Csikszentmihalyi (Ed.), *Applications of Flow in Human Development and Education: The Collected Works of Mihaly Csikszentmihalyi* (pp. 129–51). Dordrecht: Springer Netherlands.

Csikszentmihalyi, M., Rathunde, K. and Whalen, S. (1993). *Talented Teenagers: The Roots of Success and Failure*. New York: Cambridge University Press.

Edgar, D. (2009). *How Plays Work*. London: Nick Hearn Books.

Elam, K. (1980). *The Semiotics of Theatre and Drama*. London and New York: Methuen.

Esslin, M. (1965). 'Introduction'. In M. Esslin (Ed.), *Absurd Drama* (pp. 7–23). London: Penguin Books.

Fountain, T. (2007). *So You Want to be a Playwright?* London: Nick Hern Books.

Gombrich, E. H. (1966). *The Story of Art*. London: Phaidon.

Hardy, J. (1993). *Development of Playwriting Theory: Demonstrated in Two Original Scripts*. PhD, Texas Tech University, Lubbock, TX.

Haseman, B. (2012). 'Old and New Arguments for Placing Drama at the Centre of the Curriculum'. *Drama Queensland Says*, 35(1), 24–35.

Hatcher, J. (1996). *The Art and Craft of Playwriting*. Cincinnati, Ohio: Story Press.

Hayman, R. (1977). *How to Read a Play*. London: Eyre Methuen.

Herrington, J. and Brian, C. (Eds). (2006). *Playwrights Teach Playwriting: Revealing Essays by Contemporary Playwrights*. Hanover, NH: Smith and Kraus.

Ingold, T. and Hallam, E. (2007). 'Creativity and Cultural Improvisation: An Introduction'. In T. Ingold and E. Hallam (Eds), *Creativity and Cultural Improvisation* (pp. 1–24). Oxford: New York: Bergman.

Jefferson, M. and Anderson, M. (2009). 'Enter the Matrix: The Relationship between Drama and Film'. In M. Anderson, J. Carroll and D. Cameron (Eds), *Drama Education with Digital Technology* (pp. 184–201). London: Continuum.

Lassig, C. J. (2013). 'Approaches to Creativity: How Adolescents Engage in the Creative Process'. *Thinking Skills and Creativity*, 10, 3–12.

Napoleon, D. (2010). 'Can Playwriting Be Taught? 3Q4 18 Playwrights'. *The Faster Times: Theater Talk*, 13 August. Retrieved from http:/thefastertimes.com/theatertalk/2010/08/13/can-playwriting-be-taught-3q4-18-playwrights/

Nicholson, H. (1998). 'Writing Plays: Taking Note of Genre'. In D. Hornbrook (Ed.), *On the Subject of Drama* (pp. 73–91). New York: Routledge.

Norden, B. (2007). 'How to Write a Play'. *Third Text*, 21(5), 643–48.

Pfister, M. (1988). *The Theory and Analysis of Drama*. Cambridge: Cambridge University Press.

Sawyer, R. K. (2010). 'Learning for Creativity'. In R. A. Beghetto and J. C. Kaufman (Eds), *Nurturing Creativity in the Classroom* (pp. 172–90). Cambridge: Cambridge University Press.

Sawyer, R. K. (2012). *Explaining Creativity: The Science of Human Innovation*. Oxford: New York: Oxford University Press.

Selden, S. (1946). *An Introduction to Playwriting*. New York: F.S.Crofts and Co., Inc.

Smiley, S. (2005). *Playwriting: The Structure of Action*. New Haven and London: Yale University Press.

Starko, A. J. (2005). *Creativity in the Classroom: Schools of Curious Delight* (3rd ed.). Mahwah, NJ and London: Lawrence Erlbaum Associates.

Sternberg, R. J., Kaufman, J. C. and Pretz, J. E. (2002). *The Creativity Conundrum: A Propulsion Model of Kinds of Creative Contributions*. New York: Psychology Press.

Vygotsky, L. S. (2004). 'Imagination and Creativity in Childhood'. *Journal of Russian and East European Psychology*, 42(1), 7–97.

Waters, S. (2012). *The Secret Life of Plays*. London: Nick Hern Books.

Waters, S. (2013). 'How to Describe an Apple: A Brief Survey of the Literature on Playwriting'. *Contemporary Theatre Review*, 23(2), 137–45. doi:10.1080/10486801.2013.777052

Weisberg, R. W. (1993). *Creativity: Beyond the Myth of Genius*. New York: W.H. Freeman and Company.

4

Spectrum of playwriting approaches

All I am really doing is creating an environment in which people can practice their craft and try and get better at their practice and improve their confidence and improve their skill base ... improve their awareness of different techniques, and to be aware of different approaches.

I don't think it's impossible to teach playwriting and I think it's a very romantic notion that it's impossible to teach playwriting.

SIMON STEPHENS

So, on one level it is a sheer kind of raw imagination and then on the other level you have to be an architect with it. I like that it's both extremely creative and yet highly skilled. It is not enough to have just a good character, you have to have a good story and a good story is in itself a structural thing. So how you balance the two is where the work works. ... It is not enough to just have the magic, you have to have the skill too.

POLLY STENHAM

Introduction

The purpose of this chapter is to explore the resources available to teachers wanting to improve their own and their students' understanding of playwriting as an art and craft. It reviews a range of literature on playwriting pedagogy to glean from it the lessons that will improve student proficiency and understanding.

As I described in the introduction, the purpose of this book is to enable rather than restrict. As argued in Chapter 3, 'Creativity and Engagement', I consider knowledge of the craft to be liberating rather than limiting.

This chapter, and the rest of the book, outlines my response to the question, 'How can playwriting be taught?'

In 1919, Brander Matthews, in his seminal text *Playmaking*, suggested that every art must be learnt – and if it can be learnt, it can be taught (Matthews, 1919).

Writing a play is a difficult endeavour. Some of the playwriting texts argue that it may very well be the most difficult form of creative writing. Yet the occasionally well-founded interpretation that playwriting theory can be restrictive, as seen in some prescriptive playwriting 'how to texts', has resulted in a wave of newer texts that are anti-intellectual and paradoxically tentative in their didacticism, offering tips and recommendations that may or may not be useful. Alan Ayckbourn in *The Crafty Art of Playmaking* claims that playwriting is a 'purely practical [activity] that can never in the strict sense be taught' (2002, p. ix) but then proceeds to give us thirty-nine 'Obvious Rules'. He confesses, regarding his advice, that 'some of it is quite probably unique to me and contains procedures and practices that it would be highly unwise for others to try and copy' (p. ix).

But if playwriting is creating/wrighting/writing a text that 'moves bodies around ... in a space' (Gooch, 2001, p. 22), playwriting becomes imagined theatre creation, more than just text writing[1].

As such, for a playwright to learn how to create theatre, and then write the instructions, descriptions and/or recipe for that event, playwriting pedagogy will need to embrace dramaturgy. The styles and conventions, the 'isms' of dramaturgical theory, can be reimagined to enable, inspire and empower. There are great benefits to emerging writers in engaging with the spectrum of approaches, allowing them to see these techniques and conventions, styles and structures as possibilities rather restrictions.

As Gooch (2001) suggests, there is no formula for writing a play. Each new idea implies a structure peculiar to itself so that each new play is a 'fresh challenge' (p. 5). This uniqueness, however, does not mean a playwright begins each time from ground zero, in a theoretical vacuum. While there may not be rules – there are principles (Waters, 2013). The pedagogical approach outlined in this book encourages knowledge of, and interaction with, dramaturgical theory to inform a young playwright's thought and practice, to enable the development of their skills and knowledge as a dramatist. The approach also sees that with broad knowledge, students will be less likely to imitate another playwright's method or process. While we my imitate our idols, the more we know, the less derivative we can be.

Creative works exist in the context of other works and not 'in a vacuum' (McIntyre, 2012, p. 42). All plays, all artworks, belong to a continuum of practice and, 'each work is related by imitation or contradiction to what has gone before' (Gombrich, 1972). As creativity theory suggests, the new is more incremental than we perhaps admit. Knowing the domain sheds light on the range of responses open to the student faced with the 'problem' of how to convey their ideas theatrically. Kushner counsels, 'By all means … invent something new, but know where you are coming from,

---

[1]This does not suggest that the product is any less of a literary text, but one that records the playwright's imagined theatre experience rather than transcripts of dialogue between characters that is then realized as theatre by others.

who built the stage you walk out onto' (in Herrington and Brian, 2006, p. 146). Waters agrees: 'No one since Aeschylus wrote a play without seeing or reading another one' (Waters, 2012, p. 5). Any contemporary work, then, contains elements of a number of traditional principles (Smiley, 2005, pp. 92–3).

The spectrum

Unsurprisingly, the literature on playwriting contains divergent and often conflicting views on playwriting pedagogical best practice. To embrace the idea that knowledge is a resource, I have positioned the various approaches to dramaturgical and playwriting theory on a spectrum.

Following Mannfred Pfister (1988), I have described these approaches as *open* and *closed,* and explored them not as a binary but as representing a range of options, 'a smorgasbord' of devices, signs and symbols available to a playwright.

- The *closed* approach is the structure that students and teachers may regard as the 'well-made play' and focuses on plot resolution, centred on a single protagonist, struggling against both their fatal flaw and an opponent/antagonist. These plays suggest we are agents of our own fate, operating with free will. Closed plays normally include resolved dilemmas, consistent characters, and 'witty and logically built up dialogue' (Esslin, 1965) presenting a linear 'cause-and-effect' journey of character, play (via plot) and audience. A closed text tidies up loose ends.

- The *open* approach, on the other hand, informed by the experience of twentieth- and twenty-first-century avant-garde theatre makers (such as Beckett, Brecht, Kane and Crimp), includes plays and performances that choose not to resolve thematic ideas or demands of plot. They may adopt a cyclical structure, rejecting 'cause and effect' and deny the existence of an *ultimate* meaning

grounded in resolution and finality (Edgar, 2009;
Stephenson and Langridge, 1997; Waxberg, 1998).

Open texts recognize that the audience co-construct meaning
and that it is made through 1,000 subjectivities (Freeman,
2016). An open text is one that offers multiplicity and perhaps
'inexhaustibility' of meaning (Eco, 1989). This approach
embraces uncertainty without despair, values untidiness without
chaos. It will just as likely include figures or types as it will have
characters. Martin Crimp's *Attempts on Her Life*, with its
absent title character and unnamed characters, offers directors
and actors significant choices that impact the meaning created by
the performance. Sarah Kane's *4.48 Psychosis*, with its similarly
unnamed character(s), also plays around with what text is,
including numbers in non-linear formatting for example, that
allows directors to explore this play in a range of production
forms – from monologue to small or even large cast productions.

The form and/or character/figure a student chooses to
write is a product of their vision of the world (Pfister, 1988).
Pfister considers character to be as significant as plot, as one
without the other is inconceivable (p. 160). The dramatic
figure (*open*) differs from a character (*closed*), as the former
does not possess psychological realism or depth. Pfister sees
open figure conception as being enigmatic, 'due to omission or

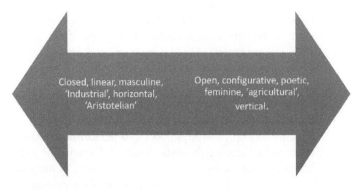

FIGURE 4.1 *Spectrum of approaches.*

contradiction, or both', whereas *closed* character conception is viewed as being explicit, consistent and fully explained (p. 180).

In terms of structure, a *closed* text with a clear 'intended meaning' that leads to a 'resolution of all open questions and conflicts and the abolition of all informational discrepancy' (Pfister, 1988, p. 95) is also a product of the student/writer's world view. The *open* text that refuses to resolve thematic ideas or demands of plot (p. 96) reflects a different view, possibly a scepticism about certainty. When considering the Aristotelian form, playwright Maria Irene Fornes recounted, 'I looked at it and started laughing because I thought: How ridiculous, that's not the way life happens. And why should one try to follow a formula that has nothing to do with life?' (cited in Herrington and Brian, 2006, p. 4).

The closed approach and the influence of Aristotle

As Fornes suggested, the source of the closed approach and the study of playwriting theory itself begins with Aristotle and *The Poetics*. For Aristotle, poetry (drama) is imitation of action; it is created by plot, through character, exploring themes (reasoning), through dialogue (diction), with music and spectacle. The text clearly argues for the primacy of plot in tragedy (Aristotle, 1996, p. 11) and that these plots should involve a good man (person) (p. 24) who experiences recognition and reversal (p. 18), thus evoking pity and fear (p. 17).

Aristotle's work has been used, often erroneously, to justify the prescriptive focus on plot and the unities of action, time and place. Yet, with a different reading, the legacy of the text could have been much broader. Equally present in *The Poetics* is the recognition that it is beautiful poetic language that *maintains* interest. He encourages a balance of clarity and 'dignity', which refers to stylistic devices or heightened language. The most important 'dignified' skill is the use of metaphor (1996, p. 36).

The long-standing influence of *The Poetics* cannot be overstated. Douhit (1990), in a review of fourteen twentieth-century American playwriting books, observes that only two of the texts did not refer directly to Aristotle (p. 19). Rowe (1968) argues that 'the fundamentals of what constitutes a drama can nearly all be found succinctly stated in the *Poetics*'. Lawson is reverential, claiming 'Aristotle is the Bible of playwriting technique' (1985, p. 9). Many of the playwriting 'how to' texts (Catron, 2002; Egri, 1960; Jensen, 1997; Selden, 1946; Smiley, 2005) write from this assumption, some structuring their approach based on Aristotle's headings. As J. L. Styan (2000, p. 12) suggests, we 'cling to Aristotle more than we know'.

While Archer (1960) suggests that Aristotle said 'you had better, rather than you must', Waters (2013, p. 138) highlights the prescriptive nature of Aristotle's tone. He argues Aristotle's recommendations are non-negotiable; 'tragedy cannot exist without plot', and the 'finest recognitions ... happen ... within blood relationships... those are the situations one should look for' (Waters, 2013, p. 138). Waters suggests that this prescriptive tone 'infiltrates and informs so much apparently neutral taxonomy' and may explain some playwrights' reluctance to engage with the theory of playwriting (p. 138).

Key lessons from dramaturgy

As a spectrum, I suggest we can learn something from all approaches. Dramaturgical texts address playwriting as a 'form of knowledge' (Waters, 2013, p. 138) and explore playwriting pedagogy by describing what a good play 'does' or 'is'. Like Aristotle's cataloguing and deconstruction of contemporary Greek tragedy, writers on the craft of playwriting analyse (their) 'contemporary' plays and describe the form by its generic parts – structure, characters, dialogue, and so on – so that novice playwrights can learn the craft through understanding how good plays have worked. Writing is thought to be learnt through meticulous dissection of contemporary and classic texts to distinguish what is fundamental to their success and what is incidental. While some of the texts include exercises, most focus on 'product' as exemplars to be *modelled*, which may be a contributing factor to the feeling that works on playwriting are prescriptive and limiting.

Playwriting is an apprenticeship

This approach to playwriting knowledge suggests that emerging writers need to understand in the 'realities' of theatre to allow them to 'analyse and evaluate [their play] in terms of common thought and practice' (Selden, 1946, p. 1). Twentieth-century 'followers' of Aristotle suggest that you need to know accepted practice before you deviate: to 'walk the road of conventional dramaturgy before [you] can safely run' (Macgowan, 1981, p. 22). The core benefit of instruction is to reveal to emerging writers how others have solved theatrical problems in the past thus shortening their playwriting 'apprenticeship' (Baker, 1919, p. iv). Albee (2009) recounted that he did just that with Samuel Beckett's texts to understand how he created his works. While this suggestion appears prescriptive, and one that encourages imitation of the well-made form, the notion that a playwright learns by understanding the works of those they admire becomes *enabling* when students are encouraged to embrace a diversity of techniques, rather than copy only one. As Klein (2012) counsels, don't steal a style – understand and adopt the thinking behind a style.

Playwriting success depends on the audience

One key idea expressed by these writers is that playwriting success means attending to the needs of the audience – who, as Edgar (2009) suggests, bring 'expectations' into the theatre that the playwright must not ignore (p. 7). Sartre agreed: 'Intentions don't count in the theatre. What counts is what comes out. The audience writes the play quite as much as the author does' (1976, p. 68).

Baker, in discussing that the dramatist should 'learn how to speak in terms his audience will understand' (1919, p. 511), anticipates a semiotic understanding, recognizing that the common language, based on agreed *signs*, is determined by audience response (Edgar, 2013). Archer (1960) regarded the audience as the holder of the 'fundamental conditions of the craft' (p. 11), and that a dramatist disobeyed them at his or her peril. Selden (1946) encourages the new playwright to examine their first draft to see if it accords with the 'traditional faiths of the spectators' (p. 61). Selden does not discourage innovation, however, but makes the playwright consider the audience's sensibilities, recommending that any breach be supported with dynamic action to 'move the audience' (p. 93). But what are these fundamental conditions or traditional faiths? As Gooch (2001) argues, the playwright balances desire for innovation against the demands of audience reception.

These expectations are both semiotic (Esslin, 1987) and narrative, illuminating this link between playwright's intentions and effective communication. The audience's expectations about story – and the structure of that story – will also influence how a playwright writes their play. As Norman (2006) argues, the audience brings with it the expectation that the 'chaos that interrupted the order at the beginning of the play will be dealt with, and the order, even if it's a new order, must return'.

The power of plot

A key aspect of the closed approach is the primacy of a linear structure. As McKean (2007) suggests, 'Most of the [playwriting] literature organises discussions on finding the shape or form of composition around a structure of beginning, middle and end'. Rowe (1968) agrees with Aristotle's edict, 'Without plot, there can be no drama at all' (p. 26). It is plot, defined as 'a unified conflict involving sufficient complications for a climactic rhythm of intensity' (p. 35), which creates and maintains suspense (p. 27). Rowe's prescriptions, reflecting those of Freytag (1900), emphasize the role of complications in increasing suspense, creating the rising action, culminating in a climax, eventually followed by falling action and resolution.

The idea is that increasingly more serious complications result in increasing action and thus increasing engagement. Selden (1946) suggests the metaphor of a 'twisting rope' – that audience engagement increases as the tension increases until, finally, the rope breaks (p. 153).

Underlying the focus on plot are assumptions about internal 'cause and effect' and the belief that plays are about 'acts of will' (Archer, 1960). Catron (2002) discusses a model for structure, paralleling both Freytag and Aristotle, which builds plot through necessary components, the 'cogs and gears' (p. 94) of a 'mechanical process' of inciting incident (p. 97), foreshadowing (p. 100), and point of attack (p. 104). While Catron argues that 'there's no suggestion here that effective playwriting must follow any particular approach' (p. 94), he divides the plot into three sections: beginning, middle and end, with recommended page lengths (p. 95).

Smiley (2005) structures his text around the six aspects found in *The Poetics* and deals with each using Aristotle's descending order of importance. He stresses the need for the conventional plot structure of beginning, developed middle and satisfying end (p. 78) and explains story as a 'pattern of causality in events' (p. 80). He does respond to the innovative twentieth-century dramatists arguing that they 'have employed the basic principles in new ways to compose their unique constructions' (p. 93). In response, Smiley describes plays as either vertical (based on conflict) or horizontal (based on tension), and argues that 'no one sort of structural movement is necessarily better than another' (p. 96). While recognizing the existence of configurative and imagist plays, the rest of the text deals with linear plot/story and psychologically complex, causally motivated characters.

Closed characterization: Psychological realism and motivated action

With more realistic and character-driven works, Aristotle's primacy of plot is challenged. As Baker suggests, it is the people in a play that determines whether it is ultimately effective or not (1919, p. 245). Archer (1960) agrees, arguing that it is character that controls plot and action exists for the sake of character. Hatcher (1996), while dedicating a chapter in his book to Aristotle and noting that his 'blueprint for a play is as useful now as it was then' (p. 21), focuses on character as 'most playwrights today believe in the primacy of character' (p. 21).

The focus on psychologically rich characters, based on a realist tradition, is found in Dunne's *Dramatic Writers Companion* (2009). This text employs Stanislavski-inspired character work to create the 'people' of the play. As 'character is the root function of scene and story' (p. xv), Dunne admits that every exercise is character exploration, as plot evolves from the characters (p. xv). Sweet (1993) suggests that the basis of drama, the action, is a manifestation of characters trying to achieve their objectives (p. 8), and that the various strategies they use form the structure of the piece (p. 29). The hierarchies and contradiction in the characters' objectives, and their attempts to reconcile their 'internal role conflict', create the realist conflict which is at the heart of a play (p. 55). Catron (2002) argues for rounded, complex characters in conflict suggesting that 'characters give shape to your play and plot is the skeleton and muscles that hold the play together' (p. 65).

These texts encourage playwrights to pay careful attention to structure and plot, to create engaging characters and to be cognizant of the audience's role in making meaning. They approach the analysis of plays, and the theory underpinning them, with precision and rigour and the strong belief in the benefit of knowing what has come before, for both efficiency and effectiveness. They provide information for those wishing to know what a 'good' play is (or at the very least, was).

To reject these texts outright appears counter-intuitive – condemning young playwrights to reinvent the wheel.

The concern here is one of 'tone'. To paraphrase Archer – even if these texts say 'you should', I encourage young writers to approach them as if they say 'you can'. In other words, if you want to make *this* kind of statement, you can use this structure/device/approach. Or, if you structure your play like this, your audience will get this message. The form or style of a piece is chosen by the impulse or idea – and you write the play the idea needs, not one that meets the categories suggested by academics (irony noted!). As Wesker (2010) argues, it is always the material that chooses the style.

This book suggests writers approach the spectrum of dramaturgical styles and conventions as a tool box, employing whatever conventions are needed to complete the task. The assumption that good playwriting is the recreation of a well-made play could be restrictive for a young playwright, but it also allows the writer to adopt these conventions if they choose. The cliché of 'learning the rules in order to break them' seems appropriate at this point.

The alternative to a closed approach

Much of what the *closed* approach suggests is both practical and effective in exploring audience expectations and is illuminating with respect to how certain plays work. But what about the student, inspired by the avant-garde plays of the twentieth century, who is attracted to forms and theatrical intent that are not served by the conventional linear approach? Fortunately for them, the Aristotelian-inspired texts do not represent the only resources available to the teacher and student and there are writers who describe, acknowledge and promote more lateral and open approaches.

Texts describing and acknowledging open approaches broaden the definition of a play and provide the playwriting student with an alternative to the standard format.

Form follows meaning – and if one doesn't exist to convey your idea, create a new one

The need to find new ways to express new ideas can be understood by exploring a key moment in twentieth-century theatre – the emergence of works considered part of the Absurdist tradition. Martin Esslin, in his introduction to *Absurd Drama* (1965), explains how forms, structures and conventions are tools; options not restrictions. Absurdist theatre, he argues, was born from the need to find a way to express each playwright's unique, revolutionary, and 'personal view of the world' (p. 14). Rather than creating new techniques, the undeniably transformative effect of these plays came from new, unusual and shocking combinations of older existing conventions (p. 15). This view positions the playwright as being in control of the conventions and that knowledge of what came before is an essential ingredient in any shift in our definition of theatre.

Plays in the tradition of the Theatre of the Absurd convey a complex pattern of poetic images (Esslin, 1965). As Hall (2000) argues, all plays worthy of our attention are poetic plays. Hall encourages playwrights to make the most of theatre's imaginative power and use all the vocabulary of the theatre – word, action, visual image and subtext – to provoke our imagination (Hall, 2000, p. 113).

Open plays and postmodernism

Castagno's *New Playwriting Strategies* promotes an approach to playwriting based on the fundamental premise that playwriting is language based (Castagno, 2001). Written in response to the perceived orthodoxy in playwriting pedagogy and playwright development, Castagno calls for a paradigm shift away from Aristotle's '"common sense dictums" [of] conflict, central protagonist and character specific dialogue' (Castagno, 2001, p. 1).

Castagno has codified and clarified the practices of a small group of 'language playwrights' to present their methods of writing 'character, language and dramatic form' (Castagno, 2001, p. 1). Influenced by a postmodern sensibility, the concepts of dialogism and polyvocality, central to the language approach, focus on meaning created by juxtaposition and represent a new approach to characterization and structure. One device, the idea of riffing, provides an approach to dialogue that highlights sound and rhythm to create moments of meaning rather than narrative information. But, like Esslin, Castagno recognizes that the language based playwrights create text that 'appears strikingly new [but] reformulates solid theatrical practices of the past' (Castagno, 2001).

New writing and the post-dramatic

Some new writing, often dubbed post-dramatic theatre, challenges many of the fundamental assumptions of traditional theatre, specifically, the focus on narrative and character, and the suspension of disbelief that entails. As part of the spectrum of new approaches to playwriting, we can see that post-dramatic theatre, by questioning of the place of text and drama in theatre, offers lessons for the student playwright even when they are writing 'dramatically'. John Freeman's *New Performance/New Writing* (2016) provides an overview of a range of forms of performance writing including live/performance art, devised works, autobiography and auto-ethnography. Embracing postmodern and post-dramatic performance conventions, Freeman encourages readers to accept the idea that reactions to, and assessments of, performance are subjective and personal.

Freeman, too, examines the new within the context of the old, outlining how, influenced by Artuad, Grotowski and Brecht, new performance eschews linear logic for a more dreamlike dynamic. Further, written text with its *intended* meaning is decentred, repositioned to be just one of the elements of performance alongside space, sound, light and so on (p. 106).

Writing in this way generates a different theatre experience. Spectators are not passively receiving the meaning of a text as interpreted by a director, but are active co-creators of individualized meaning in an *event* (pp. 32–3). This event is experienced by spectators and performers, together creating a collection of individualized reactions – his 1,000 subjectivities mentioned earlier. Rather than *more difficult*, this creates a different role for the spectators.

Freeman also reminds us that the rapidity of change in modern culture quickly turns most of the transgressive elements of new performance into conventions, tropes and expectations, suggesting all innovation is beaten by time. Exploring the challenges that new writing poses to traditional narrative structure, character and meaning, he also warns that any work that is too obtuse to communicate with a walk-in audience fails in its fundamental mission. Reminiscent of Edgar (2009), Freeman argues that practitioners interested in renewal cannot disengage from popular tastes and cultures – the audience still holds the keys.

Teaching the spectrum

For our teaching purposes, the image of the spectrum is particularly apt as it diminishes the restrictive and imitative power of 'isms': we are not demanding students to replicate such forms as realism, absurdism and so on. The spectrum positions the conventions and techniques as a kind of theatrical smorgasbord, and each individual playwright may choose their own mix of *open* and *closed* qualities depending on the central idea and vision of the play they are writing. As Gattenhof (2006, p. 13) suggests, this responds to current theatre practice that explores new conventions by drawing on a range or references, influences and disciplines, with the old coexisting with the 'new'.

This theatrical Machiavellianism does not privilege one approach over another. Ultimately the worth of the chosen conventions is judged by their ability to effectively communicate the playwrights' ideas and world view – in essence, the ends *must* justify the means. Rather than imposing a formula, these strategies and techniques are assimilated and adapted to create new 'configurations' (Castagno, 2001). A strict code of what is and is not a play, within or without a genre definition, is contrary to both playwriting reality and pedagogical best practice. As Gattenhof also suggests, when young people make theatre they 'refuse to be bound by a single aesthetic tradition' (Gattenhof, 2006, p. 13). More aligned to their experiences with episodic and devised theatre making, a broader definition of playwriting opens the students to new ways of thinking about writing for performance, including collaborative and non-language-based forms. The classroom that embraces the spectrum may empower students to see that playwriting is relevant and not *exclusively* the domain of linear and resolved action.

The classroom playwriting workshop that fosters experimentation rather than imitation will also reward student creativity and proficiency, encouraging them to create work that reflects their world view and artistic aims.

This awareness also challenges the false assumption that all new or experimental forms are 'better'. Innovation for its own sake will not ring true. But to encourage creativity, we need to approach each play as a 'new world' (Bly, 2003), and allow it to define itself, not expecting it to conform to our view of what a play 'should' be – otherwise we may miss the possibility of a 'new creation or new form evolving out of it'.

This broader definition of playwriting will also create a more inclusive environment for those writing for performance. It will embrace text and image thus addressing the hierarchy of ability often found in conventional classrooms. While traditional playwriting will still favour those with sophisticated literacy skills, a more catholic approach will allow access to others with different literacy skills and strengths.

Conclusion

The purpose of this chapter was to shed some light on the resources available to teachers wanting to develop their understanding of playwriting pedagogy. The spectrum reveals that there are really no rules and certainly no formula, just principles and tools that will help students understand how to write a text that conveys the meaning they imagine.

The chapter argues that navigating these contradictions boosts student autonomy and encourages them to treat theory as a toolkit from which to create their own style. The ideas in this chapter present teachers with a clear mandate to educate.

The spectrum approach to teaching playwriting sees knowledge as enabling and essential for innovation. The spectrum does not suggest either open or closed approaches have an aesthetic primacy, as the worth of the approach is determined by the idea, that is, by the playwright's objective. The chapter argues that there is much to learn from the range of writings on playwriting and to respond to its diversity rather than to be restricted by the models. It is the reimagining of old ideas that will generate the new.

Summary

- While there may be no rules for writing a play, there are principles.
- All creative works exist in imitation or contradiction of the works that have gone before.
- Understanding of dramaturgy will help playwrights learn how to write a play, and, therefore, help teachers learn how to teach playwriting.
- Knowledge of the spectrum of dramaturgical and playwriting theory will enable rather than stifle students' ability to write a play.

- Plays exist with in the spectrum of open and closed, and students select from these approaches the techniques and conventions that best reflect their world view and enable them to create the theatre necessary to tell their story.
- Playwriting is a dialogue with an audience – to realize their vision, playwrights need to find a common language.

References

Albee, E. (2009). 'Creativity Conversations'. In *Creativity Conversations*. Atlanta, GA: Emory University.

Archer, W. (1960). *Playmaking: A Manual of Craftmanship*. New York: Dover Publications, Inc.

Aristotle. (1996). *Poetics* (Trans. M. Heath). London: Penguin Classics.

Ayckbourn, A. (2002). *The Crafty Art of Playmaking*. London: Faber and Faber.

Baker, G. P. (1919). *Dramatic Techniques* London: Jonathan Cape.

Bly, M. (2003). 'Pressing an Ear Against a Hive or New Explorations in the Twenty-First Century'. *Theatre Topics*, 13(1), 19–23.

Castagno, P. (2001). *New Playwriting Strategies: A Language-Based Approach to Playwriting*. New York: Routledge.

Catron, L. E. (2002). *The Elements of Playwriting*. Long Grove, IL: Waveland Press, Inc.

Douhit, L. M. (1990). *The Teaching of Playwriting: As Observed in Fourteen Twentieth-Century American Playwriting Books*. Master of Arts, University of Arizona.

Dunne, W. (2009). *The Dramatic Writer's Companion: Tools to Develop Characters, Cause Scenes, and Build Stories*. Chicago: University of Chicago Press.

Eco, U. (1989). *The Open Work* (Trans. A. Cancogni). Cambridge, MA: Harvard University Press.

Edgar, D. (2009). *How Plays Work*. London: Nick Hearn Books.

Edgar, D. (2013). 'Playwriting Studies: Twenty Years On'. *Contemporary Theatre Review*, 23(2), 99–106. doi:10.1080/1048 6801.2013.777056.

Egri, L. (1960). *The Art of Dramatic Writing*. New York: Simon and Schuster.

Esslin, M. (1965). 'Introduction'. In M. Esslin (Ed.), *Absurd Drama* (pp. 7–23). London: Penguin Books.

Esslin, M. (1987). *The Field of Drama: How the Signs of Drama Create Meaning on Stage and Screen*. London and New York: Methuen.

Freeman, J. (2016). *New Performance/New Writing*. London: Palgrave Macmillan.

Freytag, G. (1900). *Technique of the Drama: An Exposition of Dramatic Composition and Art* (Trans. E. J. MacEwan). Chicago: Scott, Foresman and Company.

Gattenhof, S. (2006). *Drivers of Change: Contemporary Australian Theatre for Young People*. City East, QLD: Drama Australia.

Gombrich, E. H. (1972). *The Story of Art*. London: Phaidon.

Gooch, S. (2001). *Writing a Play*. London: A & C Black.

Hall, P. (2000). *Exposed by the Mask: Form and Language in Drama*. London: Oberon Books.

Hatcher, J. (1996). *The Art and Craft of Playwriting*. Cincinnati, Ohio: Story Press.

Herrington, J. and Brian, C. (Eds). (2006). *Playwrights Teach Playwriting: Revealing Essays by Contemporary Playwrights*. Hanover, NH: Smith and Kraus.

Jensen, J. (1997). 'Playwriting Quick and Dirty'. *The Writer*, 110(9), 10–13.

Klein, A. (2012). *Steal Like an Artist*. New York: Workman Publishing.

Lawson, J. H. (1985). *Theory and Technique of Playwriting and Screenwriting*. New York and London: Garland Publishing, Inc.

Macgowan, K. (1981). *A Primer for Playwriting*. Westport, CT: Greenwood Press.

Matthews, B. (1919). *The Principles of Playmaking*. New York: Charles Scribner's Sons.

McIntyre, P. (2012). *Creativity and Cultural Production*. New York: Palgrave Macmillan.

McKean, B. (2007). 'Composition in Theatre: Writing and Devising Performance'. In L. Bresler (Ed.), *International Handbook of Research in Arts Education*. Dordrecht, The Netherlands: Springer.

Norman, M. (2006). 'Can Playwriting Be Taught?' Retrieved from http://marshanorman.com/can_playwriting_be_taught.htm

Pfister, M. (1988). *The Theory and Analysis of Drama*. Cambridge: Cambridge University Press.

Rowe, K. T. (1968). *Write That Play*. New York: Funk and Wagnalls.

Sartre, J.-P. (1976). *Sartre on Theatre* (Trans. F. Jellinek). New York: Pantheon Books.

Selden, S. (1946). *An Introduction to Playwriting*. New York: F.S.Crofts and Co., Inc.

Smiley, S. (2005). *Playwriting: The Structure of Action*. New Haven and London: Yale University Press.

Stephenson, H. and Langridge, N. (Eds). (1997). *Rage and Reason: Women Playwrights on Playwriting*. London: Methuen Drama.

Styan, J. L. (2000). *Drama: A Guide to the Study of Plays*. New York: Peter Laws Publishing.

Sweet, J. (1993). *The Dramatists Toolkit: The Craft of the Working Playwright*. Portsmouth, NH: Heinemann.

Waters, S. (2012). *The Secret Life of Plays*. London: Nick Hern Books.

Waters, S. (2013). 'How to Describe an Apple: A Brief Survey of the Literature on Playwriting'. *Contemporary Theatre Review*, 23(2), 137–45. doi:10.1080/10486801.2013.777052.

Waxberg, C. S. (1998). *The Actor's Script: Script Analysis for Performers*. Portsmouth, NH: Heinemann.

Wesker, A. (2010). *Wesker on Theatre*. London: Oberon Books.

PART TWO

How to teach playwriting: the approach

5

How to use this book

The second half of this book outlines my approach to teaching playwriting in the classroom.

It is informed by my research into creativity and positions your students' playwriting learning (and your playwriting teaching) within the context of

- activating and mobilizing their general theatre and drama knowledge,
- challenging their (and your) beliefs about creativity and
- focusing on developing playwriting skills.

This chapter is divided into four parts:

1. the student playwright,
2. the Playwrights Wheel (exploring the playwright's skills and knowledge),
3. a discussion of the role of the teacher in the process and
4. rewriting and working with drafts.

The student playwright

Based on the understanding that playwriting skills, and creativity in general, are developed through an understanding of process and content, the approach advocated in this book recognizes that there are three distinct but interrelated areas to focus on to develop the students' playwriting proficiency.

The Student Playwright (see Figure 5.1) provides a visual representation of the aspects to consider when programming playwriting teaching and learning experiences.

An understanding of the relationship between these three components enables teachers to respond to the needs of the students and help them reach their writing potential.

The first component I call the student's *global understanding of theatre*.

This is the understanding developed from their experience of drama and theatre, of performed and written scripts and a general experience of performance. It also includes their theatre and drama knowledge and skills developed in their drama classroom.

A student's *global understanding* is their ability to make meaning from theatrical performance and dramatic text. It is their ability to read, engage with and understand theatre and drama and their ability to synthesize and express that

FIGURE 5.1 *The Student Playwright.*

understanding. As found in my research, teachers considered this understanding to be the foundation of any playwright. To this end, the Australian playwright and teacher Lachlan Philpot allocates time in his workshops to discussing work – work the students have seen, as well as the work they are writing – to allow rigorous yet supportive discussion.

The assumption that general exposure to, or immersion in, theatre will turn into an ability to create theatre is problematic. Experiencing theatre does not immediately turn into understanding. And, similarly, when students were able to interpret and deconstruct dramatic and theatrical works, they are not immediately able to create them. Students need to discuss and unpack their ideas to turn experience into knowledge. So, while necessary, exposure to theatre was not sufficient preparation for playwriting.

It became clear that students did not naturally make the link between the skills learnt in a drama class and the skills needed to write theatre. Many of the lessons that students learn through improvising, especially to do with the structures and techniques that keep a scene engaging, need to be revisited and reframed to assist their writing of drama. Their experiences of the elements of drama in workshop, for example, may not automatically inform their writing.

What this means for the classroom is that teachers need to remind students that playwrights make theatre – they write an imagined performance – and while they need to leave scope for the directorial/design team, they are writing for actors to move about in time and space. Highlighting the link between workshop activities (devising and improvising) and writing for performance will help students access the energy of improvisation in their writing.

Further, to build their creative capacity and creative confidence, students need rigorous exposure to the domain, which means exploring a broad range of genres and forms in their drama workshops. So, when teaching styles and conventions within genres, teachers can explicitly discuss the idea of a writing 'palette'. That, like a painter and their range of available colours, brush strokes and forms, playwrights choose theatre conventions, styles and forms to create a certain type of audience engagement.

The second area of focus for teaching and learning is the *student's playwriting literacy*: their understanding of the language of plays and theatre semiotics.

This goes beyond 'understanding' and refers to the student's ability to think conceptually, to develop and transpose their idea into theatrical metaphors and to create motif and symbol. It is the understanding of the language and vocabulary of sign vehicles (Elam, 1980) that enables the student to turn their idea or vision from a concept to a performable text.

The image of vehicles is important here – as it reminds them that their words convey ideas, characters and moods and are not an end in themselves.

It involves the students knowing how to control the elements of drama in the temporal reality of the stage: dialogue, setting, suspense, subtext, conflict, complications and relationships, and how to convey that through their writing.

Students' playwriting literacy is their ability to take their understanding acquired through interpreting drama and theatre and understanding *how* that meaning was made and then being able to create their own dramatic or theatrical works.

In terms of creativity, it is the skill of transference – being able to apply skills and understanding acquired in one area to another. The core work of this book is to provide exercises that develop skills in meaning making. Like a musician practising scales, the book focuses on developing playwriting literacy through writing exercises that develop students' general dramatic writing ability as well as providing exercises targeted on solving specific problems in the writing process.

The third facet I have called their *idea, vision or concept.*

This is the students' vision for the play, the ideas they want on explore, the world they want to create, and the impetus for writing. For some students, it begins with an image or concept for a theatrical moment, which then needs ideas, characters and plot to create a full audience experience. For other students, it begins with issues or thematic concerns – a burning opinion or passionately held position that motivates the playwriting. This, too, needs to be developed into a 'dialogue' of ideas, action and situations to generate audience engagement.

In a conventional approach, the initial idea is what many teachers would call the 'creative' aspect of the process – and something they feel ill-equipped to approach. This book works on the premise that the creative process requires scaffolded teaching and learning about and for creativity, to ensure students begin well and develop the skills to continue, creatively solving the problems they encounter in the writing process. Creativity and creative choices are part of each phase of the process, from the first idea to the final draft.

The method outlined in this book understands that students approach writing a play from a variety of perspectives. The activities encourage teachers to respond to the specific interests of the student, tailoring the teaching and learning to provide the most effective access point for their writing. To this end, I have created the *Playwright's Wheel*.

This wheel responds to the variety of access points for those beginning to write a play. With each segment representing a potential place to start the playwriting process, it allows for both circular and linear approaches. While you can begin the process from any part of the circle, a writer eventually needs to address each aspect. As writing a play involves multiple drafts, the student will make their way around the circle (or across, if that suits) several times, revisiting each segment to realize their play.

That is, the student who begins with a theme or issue will still need to create a world with people in it and have them act on each other, perhaps in symbolic ways. And a student who begins with a desire to write a backward structured play, or one who begins with the image or symbol, will similarly have to find characters and thematic ideas for their work.

Teachers can sequence their teaching and learning activities to target their particular students and context. For example, a linear approach may be useful in a secondary classroom situation, where the components or segments (and therefore chapters) can be approached sequentially, beginning with the idea and moving through action to character, etc. A more lateral approach might be more effective in situations based on independent study, allowing a teacher to tailor a specific programme that responds to the students who wish to create less realistic or conventional theatre. (Of course, the opposite may well be true – depending on the particular skill and experience level of your students.)

The segments of the wheel have provided the structure for the book as a whole.

All chapters will begin with a discussion of the concepts and/or key theoretical ideas often with examples from plays that illustrate the point, followed by focused activities to develop that specific skill. These activities are designed to be equally effective for a workshop or classroom context and for

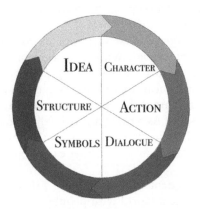

FIGURE 5.2 *The Playwrights' Wheel.*

individual study, where they may be completed in preparation for teacher–student discussion.

The segments of the wheel

1   *Teaching the idea*: After considering what a play 'is' and what it can do, this chapter explores idea and premise as the core of playwriting. It encourages teachers to spend greater time on discussing and researching the student's idea to develop their views/ perspectives on their chosen topic and develop their unique voice.

2   *Creating character*: This chapter explores the theory of characterization and relationships and the connection to style and form. It looks at the different functions of realistic characters and dramatic figures and the impact on audience experience.

3   *Generating action*: This chapter explores dramatic action – the 'what' of the play. It discusses the relationship to characterization and the importance of action as vehicles for the ideas of the play. The chapter explores the relationship between action and dialogue and their interconnection, that is, action as dialogue and dialogue as action.

4   *Writing dialogue*: This chapter discusses the key ideas that underpin the writing of dialogue, for example, the natural voice versus the stylized voice, exposition and action, character voice, etc. It encourages students to develop their dialogue writing skills in parallel with research and idea development in the early stages of writing their play. Similar to scales in music, this encourages students to develop skills in parallel to thinking about their play.

5 *Story structure*: This chapter explores the range of approaches to structure available to writers and examines how these conventions can be reinvented and manipulated. It discusses the temporal nature of the theatre experience and the functions of structure beyond storytelling.

6 *The poetic*: This chapter explores how to create depth of meaning through symbol and motif, using verbal, visual, aural and structural devices. This chapter examines the relationship of the poetic to characterization, structure and dialogue. It explores the theatrical experience and the relationship between content and style.

The remaining chapters of the book explore the practicalities of the refining process and preparing the work for performance, with a focus on the collaborative nature of creativity and the benefits of workshop performances. The book concludes by exploring the lessons from playwriting practice that can inform teachers' approaches to creativity in a range of classroom situations.

Approaching playwriting in the classroom or workshop: Teacher as dramaturg

The approach suggested by this book encourages teachers to rethink their role in this creative activity and rethink the teacher–student dynamic. The passive observer, who lets creativity 'emerge' and then corrects the mistakes, actually stifles creativity.

My suggestion is that we see the teacher not as a critic, someone who highlights flaws to be remedied, but as a dramaturg, one who builds on potential and identifies possibilities. The teacher should understand 'how meaning is made' (Aston and Savona, 1991) as well as how to scaffold learning to develop students' creativity skills and playwriting proficiency. It encourages teachers to understand how to empower students to know 'what to do when they do not know what to do' (McWilliam, 2008, p. 266).

The model also encourages teacher empowerment through fostering their increased knowledge and pedagogical skill.

The teacher as dramaturg role is fundamental, and is explained best by thinking about where the teacher is positioned. Where does the teacher 'sit' in the theatre when they engage with the play: in the audience as a critic, or backstage with the writer? If the student perceives the teacher as the critic, they will see the teacher as the one who can tell them what is wrong with their play and how to fix it. Starko (2005) describes two types of feedback: *controlling*, which positions the teacher as arbiter of good and bad, and *informational*, which encourages autonomy by providing information on what is successful. Informational feedback enables students to be in charge of organizing and evaluating their own learning. The dramaturgical model, offering informational feedback to students, enables access to knowledge of how to improve, refine and develop their work, allowing *them* to gauge its effectiveness. The best-case scenario is that the teacher takes on the role of an experienced and knowledgeable practitioner who guides the student, adding the insight, knowledge and experience absent in the student (i.e. a dramaturg). This teaches the students how to write a play as much as helping them realize their current project.

The mystical assessment of a play's success, that 'if it works, it works', results in an unnecessarily 'powerless' process for both the student and the teacher. In addition, if most feedback takes the form of annotated drafts, rather than discussion after workshop performances (see Chapter 12), then the primacy of the teacher is reinforced.

Playwriting pedagogy often sees the teacher take on a passive role that establishes the dynamic that asks the students to 'write something' and then present it to the teacher who will 'tell them if it is any good'. This teaching and learning intervention resembled the practice common in playwriting pedagogy of negative instruction (Archer, 1960). Teachers, by highlighting errors and identifying places for improvement, become problematizers, who focus students on what they cannot do or have not done.

By problematizing, the teacher unconsciously returns the teacher–student learning dynamic to a transmission mode; the student sees the teacher as the critic knowing how the play should be written and that the student would gain approval, in the form of marks, when the play accords with the teacher's feedback. At its worst, it places the student in the position of needing to come across to the teacher's view and has the potential to lead to students turning over responsibility to the teacher. Empowering students to identify their own problems while evaluating the input from a teacher is a tension that needs to be managed in teaching for creativity. The dramaturgical model works to address this tension creating clearer roles and reinforcing the students' position as ultimate decider.

The play should then not be problematized but analysed. Smiley (2005) elaborates: 'Analysis means separating the whole into parts and studying those parts and their relationships, whereas criticism frequently amounts to adverse commentary regarding faults and shortcomings' (p. 53). Therefore, moved readings should be used to highlight the play's strengths, so the student has an opportunity to see what their text is saying, and can receive feedback from the audience and the teacher. This situation allows the teacher to comment on what the play does without being the sole arbiter of the play's success or failure. While this empowers the student, it places a new expectation on the teacher.

Increased playwriting literacy further enables and empowers the student, making them less reliant on the teacher and more able to stand above and assess their own work – to be their own dramaturg. The teacher as dramaturg metaphor, in honouring the link between a student's idea generation and final realization, protects the student's concept but supports it with their experience, understanding and generous feedback. The dramaturg position demonstrates that collaboration and knowledge empower the artist and enhance creativity without compromising the integrity of the product. The dramaturg/teacher can then contribute their theatrical experience and insight to explore the skills and knowledge necessary to realize the vision of the director/student.

The role is particularly relevant to teaching for creativity in the context of student assessment. The student–teacher dramaturg relationship mirrors the director-dramaturg relationship in a production. As the student/director ultimately makes the creative decisions and theatrical choices, the dramaturg position places the student creator as *responsible* for the work. The work produced in this collaboration belongs to the student/director (Cardullo, 2000) and, while a collaboration, the dramaturg and director have distinct roles and responsibilities, and the vision belongs to the student/director.

The dramaturg position develops the inclusive approach necessary for creativity (Craft, 2005). A feature of teaching for creativity is inclusive pedagogy, where the teacher is 'passing control back to the learner … posing questions, identifying problems and issues together and debating and discussing their thinking … as well as modelling creativity in their domain [and providing] expert knowledge and advice' (Craft, 2005, p. 45).

The dramaturgical paradigm generates a spiral of learning for teacher and student. To respond to the students developing understanding and skill, the teacher needs to develop their own knowledge, creativity skills and flexibility in teaching and learning. As a new level of sophistication is attained, the teacher and student develop new skills and acquire new knowledge to address larger and more complex obstacles. This challenges the teacher to increase their level of understanding and skill to elevate the student further and strive for personal excellence. As teachers are lifted by the spiral of learning, they enrich their pedagogical knowledge, experience and flexibility, rather than relying on existing knowledge for a reactive point-of-need problematizing. The new levels of proficiency, aesthetic and pedagogical, equip the teacher to respond to the needs of students across a range of teaching and learning situations.

Writing and rewriting: Finding the gold

The dramaturgical approach leads to a positive, rather than problematizing lens. Informed by their understanding of creativity, students evaluate the worth of their ideas or the effectiveness of their writing by how well they are realizing their creative vision.

A metaphor I use here is the difference between alchemy and panning for gold. A mystical approach to creativity sees creativity as magical – turning lead to gold. But the approach I suggest is to produce work, search for gold, and then refine it further. The students, through completing the writing exercises and/or writing drafts, generate ideas and then sift through their work to find the gold – ideas, aspects and/or words worth keeping. Hilary Bell explains what she looks for when looking back at her drafts:

> It's often the bits that surprise me [where I think] that didn't sound like me – I didn't know I thought that. Things that are slightly shocking or provocative – they are the bits that I think are the stepping stones into the play and need to be encouraged, brought out, connected, somehow preserved but made more of and the stuff around them might be the obvious speeches, the boring stuff or the fluff or the clichés.

The student then builds on that gold, generates more ideas, words, etc., and finds the gold again. The approach is summed up by Polly Stenham:

> I think you write your draft, you charge at something and you just write it – and then there might be a page in there or a moment or a line and you think 'that's pretty good, the

rest isn't very good but I am going to take those bits'. And then you write around that, … and then hopefully you will write one or two more good bits and then you get rid of the rest and then eventually, through this process, you have mainly good bits.

Rewriting is part of the recursive creative process – each trip around the wheel involves rewriting.

The rewriter, however, needs to wait until the writer is finished. Getting the first draft of a scene or dialogue finished without stopping to edit or adjust is important to ensure creative ideas are not quashed before they get a chance to survive.

Similarly, there is more to rewriting than tweaking word choice and punctuation. Rewriting can often be wholesale scrapping of scenes that are not working. Tim Fountain (2007) suggests a writer should bin their first draft and rewrite from memory – and that anything that doesn't make the second draft was not worth keeping. While that is extreme, it reminds the student writer that they need to be ruthless with their words and be prepared to 'kill their darlings' if necessary.

Rewriting is an aspect of the process that needs to be managed carefully and creatively by the student playwright and the teacher – the first draft is not the end, it's only the beginning. As Hilary Bell suggests, because first drafts can be pretty discouraging, the teacher needs to help students get beyond that – and that takes time and effort. The trick is to remind them that it is not fair to compare their first draft to the thirty-eighth draft of an accomplished writer. This gives them permission to write the imperfect scene and stops what Hilary calls the *high stakes* of writing from paralysing them.

Conclusion

There is a tension between allowing creative freedom and providing the necessary scaffolding for students to develop their creative capacity.

The approach suggested in this book encourages teachers to adopt a dramaturgical position, to embrace the role of engaged pedagogy, involving scaffolding learning, exposing students to new ideas and knowledge and providing feedback on the efficacy of their work. This gives primacy to student ideas and gives them responsibility for their creative progress. The teacher/dramaturg positions the student/writer as the creative innovator. Repositioning the teacher as a dramaturg, one who can build the potential, identify possibilities and not merely highlight flaws, allows the vision/play to be analysed not problematized, provides informational (not controlling) feedback, and allows students to stand above their work and be their own dramaturg.

The new paradigm supports the student's artistic decisions with knowledge and skills. By recognizing that creative works are generated in the context of collaboration, with others, and with ideas, teachers are given permission to intervene. As the objective of creativity is empowerment, a dramaturgical model empowers students to evaluate the effectiveness of their own work, diminishing the role of teacher as problematizer and solution finder. Reimagining the position of the teacher may allow our students to create beyond their current imaginative and creative capacity and inspire our educators to teach *for* creativity, *with* creativity and *about* creativity.

Summary

- Playwriting pedagogy will be more effective if it responds to three aspects of the student playwright:
  - their general understanding of theatre,
  - their specific playwriting skills and
  - their skills in idea generation and analogical/ metaphoric thinking.
- The playwriting teacher can structure their teaching and learning strategies around the sectors of the playwright's

wheel – and use them as a variety of entry points into the process.

- The teacher will be more effective if they adopt the role of dramaturg rather than critic and aim to provide feedback that generates ideas rather than problematizes.

- Writing and rewriting will be more engaging and effective if the student is helped to find the gold.

- First drafts are allowed to be bad, allowing students to sift through and find the ideas that inspire them rather than just identifying errors and inadequacies.

- The teacher as dramaturg role allows students to develop their own skills and understanding to enable them to collaborate and retain ownership and engagement.

References

Archer, W. (1960). *Playmaking: A Manual of Craftmanship*. New York: Dover Publications, Inc.

Aston, E. and Savona, G. (1991). *Theatre as Sign System: A Semiotics of Text and Performance*. London and New York: Routledge.

Cardullo, B. (2000). 'Enter Dramaturgs'. In B. Cardullo (Ed.), *What Is Dramaturgy?* (pp. 3–11). New York: Peter Lang Publishing.

Craft, A. (2005). *Creativity in Schools: Tensions and Dilemmas*. London: Routledge.

Elam, K. (1980). *The Semiotics of Theatre and Drama*. London and New York: Methuen.

Fountain, T. (2007). *So You Want to be a Playwright?* London: Nick Hern Books.

McWilliam, E. (2008). 'Unlearning How to Teach'. *Innovations in Education and Teaching International* 45(3), 263–9.

Smiley, S. (2005). *Playwriting: The Structure of Action*. New Haven and London: Yale University Press.

Starko, A. J. (2005). *Creativity in the Classroom: Schools of Curious Delight* (3rd ed.). Mahwah, NJ and London: Lawrence Erlbaum Associates.

6

Teaching the idea

I think for an artist to think about where they are getting their ideas from and to take responsibility, for me, is more interesting than having the romantic notion of genius or ... ideas coming from the ether.

SIMON STEPHENS

I think back to the idea – it is okay to start with a bad idea. ... There are no terrible ideas, it's what you do with the idea. There are wonderful ideas that just excite everyone..., but they are hard to find – so I think it is okay to start with any idea – [but] it has to excite you.

HILARY BELL

I will do exercises to generate material and generate ideas – I won't comment on their world view, I will encourage them to look and observe, and if there is something they want to say, here are some tools to do so.

VANESSA BATES

Introduction

Writing a play, as either a classroom task or as an assignment, presents the young writer with questions common to all writers:

'What do I want to write about?'

and

'What kind of play do I want to write?'

This chapter explores ways to help students find and then theatricalize an idea; turning a concept, a thought or an opinion/position into a complete vision for the stage.

This chapter is structured around the belief that playwriting, as a creative process, involves phases and stages – including initial hunches, 'thinking', researching, learning, idea generation, experimentation, idea evaluation and refinement – and that a teacher can scaffold teaching and learning experiences to develop student proficiency across all these phases. The initial germ of an idea – often mistakenly considered the only creative part of writing – is actually the beginning of a continual longer creative process and is really only complete when the play is realized. Throughout this process the student's idea will develop and modify, generating further creative problems for the student to solve.

There is great benefit in approaching the ideation phase with scaffolded teaching and learning processes and activities to generate, test and refine ideas. As Hilary Bell suggests, the worth of an idea is really what you do with it.

Rather than expecting a good idea to arrive fully formed, encourage students to identify several possibilities and sift and mould and 'mull' over them to see how they develop. Encourage them to read and write and research and play, and to wrestle with ideas – giving them time to explore before asking them to settle. As Lachlan Philpott suggests, you need to allow time for thinking.

This chapter encourages teachers to focus on idea generation in an active rather than mystical passive way. Ideas are
made, not found. It explores the play's idea from theoretical
and practical perspectives and provides knowledge and skills-
based activities to broaden students' understanding of genre,
styles and forms. The more they know, the more they have to
play with to create something new.

The theory and practical activities described in these
chapters are as much for the students as for the teacher – for
you to read and digest and modify to complement your existing
understanding and teaching approach and to share and co-
create with your students. To this end, I address the teacher
in the body of the chapter – where I talk about teaching and
learning – and the student when outlining writing exercises.

First thoughts: What kind of play?

Initial discussions should focus the student on seeing playwriting as a theatrical and dramatic conversation with the audience.

The most straightforward way to begin the playwriting process with a student is to ask them what it is that is motivating
them to write a play (this answer might be 'because we have to'!).

But the question is still valid. Specifically, why a play and
not a film or a short story? This focuses the student on what
plays do well and what possibilities they offer.

The conversation may begin with the following questions:

What makes a good play?
What plays have you seen that have been powerful,
    memorable, interesting?[1]
What can a play do that a film, novel or poem cannot?

---

[1]The dilemma will be if they respond that they haven't seen/read many plays.
Despite what we do as drama educators, my experience suggests that is the
most likely scenario. So, they need to see as many plays as they can; to read
as many plays; to put on a few plays. This of course is easier to do in some
teaching and learning contexts than others.

These reflective questions not only provide teachers with an understanding of the student's global understanding of theatre and their peculiar interests, it also focuses the student on the possibilities of the form, which may, in itself, generate ideas.

To focus more students on writing for the theatre, for an imagined and future audience, ask them the following questions:

- What kind of play do you want to write?
- What kind of audience experience do you want to create?'
- What do you want to write about?
- What do you want the audience to take away from the play?
- What do you want them to feel, think or do once they leave?

These are imaginative rather than dramaturgical questions. They help you understand where your student is and what they will need and how best to scaffold the teaching and learning experiences. They ask students to visualize what they think is possible with playwriting – so allow/encourage big ideas. Their answers need not be practical or even possible at this stage – it is about finding out where they are and what they know.

Their responses will also help them understand what kind of play is needed to convey the ideas they are interested in and how to create the theatrical experience they imagine. It will generate and focus thoughts about the kind of dialogue they will write, the form and structure of the play and its scenes, and the actor–audience relationship that will best serve their concept. And if they can articulate these in some depth *they* can begin to consider what will interest them and motivate them to complete the difficult writing process. It will also suggest the kind of dramaturgical assistance they will need and what ideas and suggestions they will respond to and what will inspire them.

All these considerations remind the student that they are creating theatre – that they will write a play for performance –

and not just characters in conversation. It focuses students on the audience, on creating an experience for people in the theatre.

These questions also encourage the students to see playwriting as a process that values thought and reflection, as well as knowledge of form and structure.

While often stressful for teachers experienced with procrastinating students, reflection and thinking before you write are essential. Keen to get started, too often students get a whiff of an idea and begin writing without knowing where they want to go and the results can be problematic. That is not to say early writing isn't a possible approach but young writers need to focus on audience experience. The process begins well when a student imagines a play that 'acts' on an audience, creating theatre experiences that move or change an audience in some way. A good play will create feelings to inspire curiosity and generate insights. A play creates an experience that explores ideas in ways that affects an audience emotionally or viscerally: we want the audience to squirm and gasp and ponder and laugh. Thinking early also helps students to establish the rules of the world they are imagining and, therefore, create a coherent vision.

Consider these clarifying questions:

- How do you want the audience to participate in the action of the play? What do you want them to do?
- How do you want them to respond? (This will help you look at the central question of form.)
- How big is the play? How many characters? How big is the space? How intimate?
- What structure do you think it will need? Linear episodic or linear narrative? Disrupted episodic or disrupted narrative?[2]
- What type of dialogue do you want to create? Naturalistic, poetic, stylized, brittle?

---

[2]You may not use these terms with your students but you will help them realize their ideas through your understanding of them – the dramaturg again.

For example, an intimate observation of a family dynamic – asking questions about what happens in our most intense relationships – might need a small cast, limited settings and an intimate stage. An exploration of how power structures are manipulated to hide greed and malice – coming from a question of casual cruelty might suggest a large cast, episodic structure with technical wizardry. These questions also foreshadow the need for students to consider each segment of the playwright's wheel, not just the one they feel is their strength.

Idea and opinions

The next step in this approach is to ask what their play is going to be about[3]. While the motivating idea can take many forms, such as an image or a character, this chapter explores issues, opinions or perspectives as the starting point of writing. This entry point focuses on how a play interrogates a theme. As discussed, at some level all plays explore the big issues. Taylor (2002) suggests that plays are a forum of ideas. The playwright writes a play because they have a concern they want to discuss, a question they want to ask or a dilemma they want to share with an audience. As a forum, a play is a dialogue of ideas – for the characters and for the audience. There should be a scope for an audience to formulate their own response – even if it is silent or visceral, an audience will need to participate to be engaged.

While this approach appeals most to students who reflect upon the world and enjoy interrogating the issues that perplex them, all playwriting encourages (perhaps even requires) a desire to explore what it means to be human and to understand the world.

---

[3]As with many of these activities they are more correctly parallel rather than linear, but for the purposes of a structured teaching and learning programme they can happen in this order. For example, realistically, the idea chooses the form.

A discussion of a significant 'idea' gives a play the insight necessary to keep it relevant to an audience. As Mac Wellman (in Herrington and Brian, 2006) suggests, a great play causes the audience to *reflect* on their world and their place in it. And through a play's tendency to encourage empathy, playwriting offers young people a positive, productive and outward looking outlet for their questions about themselves, their identity and 'what it all means'.

To do that, we encourage students to reflect on what they believe in and to explore the ideas and assumptions within their passionately held beliefs. We encourage students to find an idea they are deeply invested in, to find that concept that puts a metaphorical fire in their belly. Rivera (cited in Herrington and Brian, 2006) talks about students choosing ideas that are vital to their existence, while Marguiles (cited in Herrington and Brian, 2006) suggests the topic needs an intensity that captures their imagination. For some, like Gooch (2001, p. 6), the idea is the most important aspect of the play that guides all the emotional, intellectual and sensual choices involved in writing the piece. The idea determines all the other decisions about form, action and character.

At the root of all drama is the process of making sense of the chaos of existence. How we organize our ideas, and try to bring structure to our understanding, influences the devices we select and how we manipulate them to organize and structure the events on the stage.

But there is a tension between clarity of idea and richness of theatre. A play is a three-dimensional live experience of characters in time and space – and not an essay, speech or pamphlet. The play will communicate something but the more complex the questions the less they respond to simple answers.

This focus on theme is not without its critics. As Spencer (2002, p. 154) argues, there are other ways to consider the relationship between idea and writing a play, suggesting a theme need not be clearly articulated before you begin. These approaches will be discussed in subsequent chapters.

Getting started

While some writers argue that you can't teach someone to have ideas (Gooch, 2001) there are strategies a teacher can implement that help a student convert opinions into premises, interests into situations and people into characters (i.e. ideas for play).

As Catron (2002) offers, a great way to start is to get students to identify their beliefs and organize them. Simon Stephens asks his playwriting students to consider the fundamental questions: What does it mean to be human? What makes us different from other animals? These questions ask the emerging writer to consider what is essential about humanity. At the beginning of the writing process, students might come with a theme or an issue: racism or suicide or violence. But often that concept is too *big* and will not lend itself to a theatrical expression. They might say 'I want to write something about injustice'. But this theme needs to be refined – it needs to be actioned.

Student playwrights choose their theme as a response to their experiences and the conclusions or perceptions about human behaviour that these experiences suggest. The teacher's role here is to bring that idea down and focus on the specific fundamental human struggle the theme is going to explore.

Ask the student the following questions:

- What makes you furious?
- What brings you joy?
- What issues distress or concern you?
- What makes you hopeful and energized?
- What is it about these concepts that engages you (or why)?
- What aspect of 'life' does it help you understand?

As we discussed in the introduction, a play needs conflict and complications, so the idea must be one that allows for multiple perspectives and conflicting opinions.

Statement of purpose

Despite suggesting that a play is a dramatic question, when working with young writers asking them to clarify their idea can bring focus to their process and scaffold their writing to help them stay on track. Having an idea of the destination or objective of the piece allows them to evaluate how well they are going. Encouraging the student to strive for clarity – to make their idea specific – encourages them to focus again on what they want the audience to take away from the experience – more than just wanting the audience to 'think about' their issue. Remind them that any heavy handedness or unsubtlety can be addressed in subsequent drafts.

One way to increase a student's clarity in their process is to ask them to express what can be called the 'statement of purpose'. This statement is the motivating objective – the idea or central experience to be explored and communicated in the play. Polly Stenham calls this her 'line of inquiry'. Defining the fundamental[4] observation or question in their play will help the students evaluate the effectiveness of each new scene or action. The statement of purpose should be a short clear sentence.

Egri (1960) calls this the premise of the piece. A premise is the basic idea of your scene or play – it is the core of your idea, the thing you wish to explore and to understand or convey. It is the motivating objective – the idea or central experience to be conveyed explored and communicated (Egri, 1960). It becomes a statement of purpose when it is focused into a statement or a question. A premise has a clear syntax and structure. Egri (1960) argues that a premise should start with a character trait or quality, then explore a conflict or complication (in a clear and active verb) and end with an observation or 'position'. An example is the premise 'Bitterness leads to missed opportunities.' The strength of the premise is

---

[4]But not declarative or didactic.

the implicit movement written into the idea – there must be change for this premise to be realized.

I encourage students to express their statement of purpose in the form of a debating topic, such as 'That violence breeds resentment' or 'That family love can cripple'.

It might be the play's fundamental moral question but phrasing it as a statement that is open to argument frames the ideas as one that has two sides and the playwright needs to understand both to create an engaging play.

The student then writes the core premise or statement of purpose for their play on a piece of paper and places it in a prominent place where they write – on a post-it on their screen, or as a title page in their note book. This gives their work a destination and a lens to evaluate each additional scene. They ask, 'Is this scene bringing me closer to the premise? Does it further my statement of purpose?' It gives the student an objective to judge each moment on how well it is exploring the core issue. And it provides voluntary parameters on the work to keep the play coherent.

This approach works well for realist, dramatic playwriting. The statement of purpose can be described as the play's super-objective and each scene has a smaller discreet objective, what Simon Stephens calls the 'game' of each scene. However, this thinking works equally well for non-realist, episodic or post-dramatic pieces, helping to define the intended experience for the audience and to allow the playwright to evaluate the effectiveness of each moment or episode.

It is better that a premise evolves rather than vacillates. Substantial time working through the ideas at the beginning will be beneficial to the overall writing process. As I encourage teachers, 'An hour here will save ten at the end.' The clarity also ensures the audience is not left unsatisfied because the play didn't know what it wanted to do – say – be.

Egri (1960) argued that writing a play required the playwright to take sides. And while the playwright needs to be clear on their underlying or overriding purpose, they may never mention it. This echoes an idea voiced by Jose

Rivera (cited in Herrington and Brian, 2006) that there is a paradox surrounding clarity of idea and the openness of a dramatic question. The play can be mysterious for an audience but cannot be confusing. A playwright needs to make decisions about what it means even if they keep those decisions ambiguous for an audience. Despite many young playwrights' belief in postmodern openness of meaning, a good play doesn't leave it up to the audience to decide what the play 'is'. The student writer needs to know the answer behind the mystery.

This does not mean that there can't be ambiguity within a plays narrative or thematic meaning. Much new writing, influenced by post-dramatic and postmodern aesthetics, does in fact ask the audience to create much of the meaning (Freeman, 2016). As Lachlan Philpott suggests, 'Fixing and clarifying and whittling [a play] down until any sort of ambiguity or uniqueness has been sanded away' is stifling new writing and new theatre forms.

These tensions are often hard for a teacher to manage. While students perhaps like to err on the side of ambiguity, this is more often a result of a lack of skill rather than a desire not to be dogmatic. This is where mastery of the craft and clarity of idea can help teacher and student create the play the student imagines.

Discussion and idea generation

Continue the process by opening discussion with the students about their views and attitudes, passions and concerns. Spend time working through what they are passionate about, helping them become more aware of what they think and what 'events' or people made them think that.

Focus their ideas through the parameters of the project. How long is the play going to be? The teacher (as dramaturg) can help the student understand the task well enough for the student to evaluate if their idea is big enough or small enough for the play they need to write. This could then prompt research into the short play form so the idea develops in the context of the possibilities and limitations of the form and task.

Similarly, encourage students to think metaphorically about the concepts that will be their play's text and subtext. By asking the student to think about what their ideas suggest in terms of an image, a sound, a motif, a character, a situation, you keep them thinking 'laterally' and analogically while their idea is still forming.

This discussion would suggest further research and imagining. The teacher, as dramaturg, would then provide links to texts with the same theme, works of art that explore these ideas or resonate with the mood or atmosphere that these ideas suggest. Emphasize the importance of research to ensure they have an informed understanding of the issue – and that they can formulate an *authentic* position – rather than an unexamined opinion.

Their initial creative responses to these ideas can involve a range of media. In addition to collecting images and music that represents their feelings on an issue, they would also create short pieces of writing that will begin to form the seeds of the bigger play, writing such as character backgrounds, monologues, out-scenes, etc. that develop details that may or may not appear in the text.

Hilary Bell explores how asking pointed questions can help the student writer find what is interesting in an idea:

Say it's about a girl whose boyfriend dumps her – banal – but everybody goes through it, what did she do to drive him away? How can she get him back? Who did he leave her for? Once you get them curious, asking questions and letting it be a bit of a bread crumb path [it can] go somewhere totally different to where you started out.

Using a journal activity to help students to articulate and *own* their views might be a good place to start. Self-reflection is a good skill for a playwright and needs to be exercised and practised.

Writing exercise: Idea creation

Part 1

Answer these questions in your writing journal:

- What is something that you are passionate about?
- What is something that really troubles you?
- What makes you furious?
- What makes you blissfully happy?

Focus on fury and bliss. Keep the stakes high. What puts the fire in your belly?

Part 2

Write down ten clear and direct statements that express your most passionate beliefs (adapted from Itallie, 1997).

These may be opinions that you have formed based on your experiences – but at this stage keep them general. For example, 'I believe that everyone should be free from violence.'

Now, choose one and write about the idea. Write for twenty minutes without stopping. Don't edit and don't try to be good or even worry if it seems boring and you are repeating yourself. Write for as long as you can and get passed the obvious ideas and see what fresh, new or weird ideas you can come up with.

At the end of the twenty minutes go back and read what you have written. Look for ideas that excite you as a reader and look like they could be further developed. Circle or highlight them in your text.

Now, collect images that explore these ideas and feelings and stick them in your journal.

Then, think of key words that explore your feelings and responses to these images and write them on post-it notes and stick them on your images.

Reflect on these ideas – perhaps for a few days/overnight or after lunch, depending on the teaching and learning context.

Now, write a few statements that pin down a few of the ideas that emerged from this activity. They could start as questions but try to turn them into statements. They need to be clear, but open for exploration, imply opposing positions rather than one sided and 'closed'. Look for big ideas rather than specific ones. Things like:

Violence comes from fear
or
Honesty and truth are more important than success.

These will act as potential statements of purpose for your play. The images might suggest characters, locations even situations. The songs may suggest mood or inspire story.

Now, write for another ten minutes on what these ideas suggest and where the play might go.

Voice

Once students have articulated their views and opinions, they need to bring something original to the topic. The goal for students is to develop and then articulate an authentic voice. This means being true to their reflections on experience and not trying to replicate the experiences or views of others. The first resource a playwright (of any age) draws on is their own understanding, capacity and imagination (Jester and Stoneman, 2012, p. xi).

Originality

As Gooch (2001, p. 17) suggests, there is the expectation that playwrights will have something striking and original to say. For young playwrights this originality is achieved through a deep reflection on what they believe and an authentic exploration of their perspective.

But the pursuit of originality is a paradox. Inspired by two ideas from creativity theory (see Chapter 3) a teacher can encourage 'original' playwriting, and thus an original student voice, first, through recognizing the worth of little 'c' creativity, and second through valuing the creativity involved in replicating a form and style. Creating an artefact – a play – that did not previously exist, based on their perspectives on the world, is an impressive expression of creativity and originality.

The play the student writes will be original because they haven't written this form, about this topic or about these characters before. Also, if they are true to their *theatrical* vision (and not try to copy someone else's) their work will be authentic. Further, if they improvise and 'play' within the form they are using, then it will be original. Improvising within the parameters of form and style, to even work outside them, will see their voice emerge. The creative thinking required in making the complex choices and decisions in the playwriting process, including navigating the emerging problems encountered as the play evolves, represents significant creativity that students and teachers can recognize and celebrate.

Authenticity

Audiences come to a play to see or hear insights into experiences of life. Wesker (2010) calls this the playwright's perception, defining it as intelligent reflection on the human experience. Simon Stephens (2016) suggests that fundamentally *all plays* explore what it means to be human.

Our unique experiences of and in the world – intellectual, emotional and visceral – create our attitudes and beliefs. Our conclusions about what the world means are made through reflecting on *experience*. Simon Stephens suggests that this includes everything that happens to us, including – but not limited to – the books we read, the music we listen to and the plays we see. Students are often told to write what they know but that is limiting. Encourage them to write what they know, what they can imagine, what they want to understand and what they feel.

To be a playwright we need to reflect on our experiences and come to some conclusions and offer some insights that are of relevance to others and, perhaps, be of universal significance.

Focusing on human experiences keeps the idea theatrical – reminding students that a play is about people in a situation and in conflict.

And, as will be discussed later, these insights are also aesthetic – a student playwright's voice is also 'heard' in how these insights are expressed. For a playwright, perception, their intelligent reflection, includes their skill in the playwright's craft, including their choice of techniques and conventions to convey the ideas and needs of their theatrical world.

It is both the ideas and the way they are conveyed that is the personal signature of the writer.

Engaging and enriching insights into the human condition – as we see from Polly Stenham's debut play *That Face* – are available to the young. *That Face*, written when she was nineteen, explores a dysfunctional family dynamic, perceptively depicting the destructive power of relationships and the potential for cruelty inherent in familial bonds. Commenting on the British class system, emblemized in the opening scene in the boarding school, the play interweaves the personal and the political. The authenticity of her insights comes from her understanding of relationships brought about by interaction with literature and theatre, as well as her reflection on her life experiences. Stenham had a rich and varied theatrical education, having experienced much great theatre in her childhood and youth. She had also studied Albee's *Who's Afraid of Virginia Woolf* and Williams's *A Streetcar Named Desire* for her final year at school – two plays that were, as she says, 'all over' her play *That Face*, even to the point that the maternal character is called Martha. These influences were the parameters in which her creative and perceptive insights flourished. The play's observations about domestic cruelty and sibling love are authentic and original.

Truth and autobiography

The relationship between a playwright's work and their life is a complex one and one worth reflecting on as an educator of young writers.

A writer is embedded in their play and writing involves some personal risk. A writer's innermost thoughts are going to come through in the work that they write (Gooch, 2001).

A playwright offers the audience an insight into their inner self, revealing their opinions and beliefs. Like all writers, playwrights invite speculation about the experiences that led to their observations and playwrights create characters that may or may not be them, or their dad or their friends. Eugene O'Neill's *Long Day's Journey into Night* was a veiled retelling of the sins of his family – so close to truth that he prevented performance of this play until after his death.

However, the processes suggested in this chapter (and book) do not encourage a retell of life events. Writing a play encourages perception, not therapy. The job of playwriting is not self-revelation; the ideas need to resonate to an audience beyond themselves. The choice of topic needs to create powerful theatre not just powerful feelings in the writer. This is not to say that young people will not work things out through their play. I don't deny that playwriting is personal work. The tension is that a play that is too close to autobiography may not include sufficient distancing devices or universal insights, but one without deep personal reflection may be inauthentic.

As I found, young playwrights mine their life experiences for their plays and can create work that reflects their central concerns in ways they are not completely aware. One of the students in my study reflected the power of playwriting to encourage self-reflection and that this was sometimes unconscious. Patricia[5] had written a non-naturalistic play and had not set out to have a message: 'I am not Brecht,' she said. However, as I read her play and discussed her motivation and process, it became evident that her play symbolized her own struggles with societal expectations and she had created a subtle metaphorization of her life and identity issues. Patricia had been unaware of the autobiographical parallels until our discussions and was very excited by the revelation that her play was the manifestation of her dilemma of 'how to be happy' and 'how to live in a world of rules'. Playwriting became a way for Patricia to make metaphors of her life experiences; creating *characters* to grapple with the dilemma of navigating the social world she seemed to not instinctively understand, and which didn't understand her. In creating these metaphors and characters, Patricia demonstrated that she did have insight into the pressures of society and the challenging chore of negotiating expectations. Her metaphor was externalizing her internal conflict. The central dilemma of the people in the world of her play was the central dilemma of her life: 'Do I want to break the rules? Do these rules have validity?'

However, as Hilary Bell suggests, only writing from their own experience not only leaves the students with little to write about, it is also an insult to the imagination. She argues:

> I think from the moment we are born we experience a huge range of emotions – we don't necessarily experience a huge range of adventures, but we have to be able to write about them.

---

[5]All student names are pseudonyms.

Simon Stephens explains a similar perspective on autobiography:

> I am not even sure [playwriting] is autobiographical
> at all. ... Really nothing that I have written has been
> autobiographical – there have been ghosts of autobiography
> and they are really only ghosts. [Writing is] imaginative
> and inventive. ... The danger ... is encouraging people to
> write their own stories and dramatize their own stories.
> [Playwrights] are drawing from their own wounds to make
> those stories – they are not writing autobiography, but their
> gesture of imagination is drawn from themselves.

Stephens suggests that, rather than being autobiographical, the
playwright draws from their 'wounds' to create metaphors,
imagined characters, situation and events.

That is not to say that the people in the student's plays
won't include aspects of themselves and the people they know.
The craft of playwriting is creating a vehicle to carry the ideas
into fiction.

Plays need the distance created by metaphor, symbol,
character and location.

Finding the vehicle: Turning an idea into a theatrical vision for a play

The next phase in the process sees the student transform
their intellectual concept and perceptive observations into
a theatrical metaphor, a theatrical vision and/or a dramatic
question.

The dramatic metaphor has two functions: It is a vehicle to
carry the ideas through 'space' to an audience while also acting
as a distancing device to protect the student.

At its simplest, the students' ideas need to be realized
in a situation – people, in relationship, in a place. Yet, an
effective vehicle will also be a metaphor, utilizing the unique

visual and verbal poetry that is live dramatic and theatrical performance.

A writer uses verbal and physical metaphor to encourage a range of reactions in the audience – visceral, emotional and intellectual. The right dramatic metaphor will affect the audience in these ways. As we experience the world as a 'body' in space, plays are representations of that embodied experience.

Even if they end up writing about their own experiences, through discussion, analysis and reflective writing, young playwrights will be able to find metaphors or situations that get to the core of these experiences and create a vehicle that allows them to speak to the universal.

Young people often express a desire to write about teenage depression and suicide. These ideas pose problems within a school setting regarding mandatory reporting and protection of child welfare. However, within this context of professional responsibility and judgement, they need not be avoided at all costs. Many students feel very passionate about these topics as they affect them *as a group*. To create a theatrical idea, the teacher can unpack these issues and can work with the student to identify what it is about the topic that is of interest. Asking 'What is it about that experience that captivates you?' or 'Why are you passionate about that?' the student may respond that, perhaps, depression causes or is caused by loss of identity, despair, hopelessness, loss of meaning – all ideas that can be transformed through metaphor into an authentic theatrical idea.

The following exercise, effective in individual, paired or whole class situations, will encourage students to be specific in their topic choice and to focus their ideas through a theatrical lens.

Writing exercise: From big idea to situation

Phase 1: Big idea

Think of all the big ideas (including 'isms') that you hate or love, and those that intrigue or perplex you. That is, ideas like cruelty, generosity, jealousy, hope, pettiness, courage, racism, etc.

Leaving four to five lines between each, write them down on the left-hand side of a page. (If you are working in groups, this could be done on a big sheet of butchers' paper.)

After each big idea, write a phrase that develops that theme further by making a statement or asking a question – again, make sure it includes a verb.

What precisely upsets or inspires you about this idea? For example, if you are angered by 'overbearing parents', the phrase would unpack the cause of that anger, such as 'parents disrespecting children' 'parent not trusting children' or 'parents ignoring children'.

Then, to develop it further, consider asking 'What causes this?' and 'Why do people act this way?' Explore motivations – what people want and how that generates action. Why do parents ignore children? (Because they are resentful of their lost freedom?)

Now, explore the consequences of these actions. What happens when parents ignore children?

This will create situations that quickly becomes about actions and reactions of people trying to get what they want.

Phase 2: Situations

If you choose one of the topics – say the idea of overprotective or 'helicopter' parents – think of specific situations where this issue might cause conflict.

Think of pairs or small groups of people who would be involved in these situations.

For example:

- Parent(s) and child (where the child asks for permission to go to a party)
- Two or more siblings (where one is allowed to go somewhere and the other isn't)
- Pairs of parents (where they discuss who is going to let their children go to the party)
- Parent and child's friend (where the friend lets the parent know they are/are not going to the party)

These situations provide parameters in which to explore the idea – grounding it in character and place.

Write out mini descriptions of the situations – who is involved, what are the relationships, where are they? That is, create the basic details for an improvisation. Now improvise/ write each situation into a scene.

(Hint: These characters and situations could form the overarching structure of an episodic class play interrogating parents and children.)

Phase 3: Getting to the core

Now we need to focus the ideas even further and to explore the issue at the core of each situation. Explore the ideas – attitudes or emotions – from the perspective of each of the characters in the situations.

So, helicopter parenting suggests ideas of respect, freedom, resentment, etc. And we need to know why each character acts the way they do and what they feel. So, from the parents' perspective, it is about trust (of the child) and fear (of the unknown) and for the child it may also be trust, as well as freedom or hope or peer pressure, identity and respect.

Write the name of the situation, the characters and their attitudes to the core issues on index cards and place them in your journal (or around the classroom).

These are the skeleton of your play.

Improvise/write a scene from each situation and mix up the objectives – Character A wants to respect but Character B is motivated by fear.

This will open up your play, evolving from one based on your 'lives' to one exploring universal concerns and situations. This process is important as it

1   makes sure your scenes are precise and subtle – not a general wash of anger and/or hurt;

2   allows you to develop scenes of negotiation – where each character has a valid place to start; and

3   creates real people in real situations struggling for something they believe in, that is, high stakes!

Creativity and imagination: Writing to find the idea

While it is not mysterious, the act of writing is still and should be *imaginative*.

The playwriting process will include moments of inspiration and insight, and the teacher can prepare the student for these moments (and how to generate more) by providing structures and exercises. The teacher's role is to scaffold the creative process so that when intuition and imagination are 'sparked' the student knows how to capitalize on these opportunities.

Teachers can provide exercises that help students generate imaginative ideas. While these activities are still based on the writer's underlying thoughts and experiences, by silencing the paralysing voice of the censor they allow and (perhaps) trick the brain into generating ideas. Just as a teacher introducing improvisation exercises to a class encourages the students to turn off the internal critic, improvised writing exercises can help 'silence' the voice that tells the student not to write a certain line because it's not cool enough or it's not clever enough. The writer too has that voice waiting to criticize early ideas.

The following activities give the students permission to be 'bad' and even encourage it. These activities offer students liberating and surprisingly productive freedom. Like many in this book, they can be undertaken in parallel with other activities and respond to the phases of the creative process. While the students focus on skill development, their ideas have the chance to incubate. The other benefit is that it keeps the student writing – creativity is enhanced by quantity. Hilary Bell encourages writing to find things out – how her characters speak, how they interact; as she says:

The actual writing can generate and stimulate ideas.

The trick is to remind students that this is practice not final product – and may not and probably won't end up in their play. Again, be wary of students falling in love with their words, because it will be harder for them to break up with them if they realize they are no longer good for their play: they need to know their words are potentially disposable.

Free writing is a way to generate lots of words that may or may not end up in the students play but will encourage students to write without censorship and then to 'look for gold'. The strict parameters within which to write, in this case time, allow the students to overcome the tyranny of the blank page. Depending on the level, this can be two to five minutes or extended to ten to fifteen for older students. The process is similar to extended improvisation where students remain in the scene for a longer than normal period of time, until they break through the barrier of self-consciousness and give in to the moment.

Writing exercise: Free writing

In this exercise, the restriction or parameter is time. You are to write for the whole time and not stop or edit or judge. You are to continue writing until the time is up.

You can write anything you want but are encouraged to start to improvise within the piece – finding rhythms or 'riffing' on ideas, words, phrases that happen.

Starters will be given – such as words or images – and you can write in any form you like – prose, monologues, scenes, etc.

Now, write for five minutes.

At the end of the time reread your words and circle ideas that are engaging, inspiring, surprising, etc., perhaps pretending you are reading someone else's work.

Focus is on what is good – look for the gold. Work from the assumption that there will be an idea that will surprise and capture your imagination. It may be a phrase, a character or an image or a symbol that interests or inspires you. Look for ideas that stand out, and may even reveal to you the images, characters and ideas they are passionate about. Circle those ideas.

Writing exercise: Structured writing

The following exercise is an example of a poetic monologue that helps you identify ideas or images that inspire you.

It is called 'I remember'.

You will write for an extended period – today eight to ten minutes.[6]

Beginning each line or phrase with the words 'I remember', write short clear sentences that are reconstructions of your memories. For example:

- I remember walking on a beach and collecting rocks – looking for circles.
- I remember catching a bus and seeing a girl with a weird bowl cut.
- I remember her becoming one of my good friends – and losing the bowl cut.

---

[6]Or maybe even twenty minutes depending on the class and experience.

Be vivid and describe the scenes as you remember the event – replaying the event in your head. The memories are not analysed or synthesized and won't be shared.

The idea is to recreate the perspective of the 'you' that had that experience – the attitudes and awareness or maturity of your much younger self.

This reminds us that we remember and imagine in 'scenes', and that memories are replayed in our minds, recreating the moments and adding imagined perspectives and motivations in the actions of others. These skills develop your writer's instincts and perceptions.

After the activity, examine the words to see what ideas were important to you and what feelings were evoked by the memories.

This is a starting point to fictionalize real moments and feelings – and helps you get to the core issue in your experiences.

Consider what ideas it gives you for scenes? How could you explore the ideas/feelings from your life but in a completely fictional situation?

Writing exercise: Guided writing

For this exercise, move to an individual spot and I will take you through this guided writing exercise.

I will start you off with a prompt and then, as you write, will introduce new ideas that you will need to incorporate into your writing, like improvising with an unknown partner.

The best thing to do is not overthink – just work it in as quickly and as simply as possible. Perhaps don't even try to craft – just write. The writing doesn't have to be good – in fact it is unlikely to be – because that is not the point.

The goal is to write to find ideas – to let the flashes of inspiration break into the writing.

The activity begins when I give you a first line – one that places character/s in the middle of something; for example:

- I just told you that...

    or

- I didn't think it would matter...

    or

- This has never happened before...

Now write, and at various intervals I will tell you what you need to include (information/actions/events), namely:

- At two minutes[7] – 'a new character enters and offers a valuable gift';
- At four minutes – something gets broken;
- Then at six minutes, a lie is revealed;
- At nine minutes, one character decides to leave, with an explanation;
- Then, at twelve minutes, a phone rings;
- At sixteen minutes, 'find an end';
- Pens down at twenty minutes.

Now, reread to find ideas, images or lines that you like. Find the gold – it may be a character or an interaction; it may be the image of one character giving another character an expensive gift, only to find out immediately after that the gift was stolen; or the recipient has already decided to leave (break up with) the giver.

Find the moments you like and reflect on why you liked them. What was evocative or engaging? Work within a process of constant creation and evaluation, sifting to find the good not to remove the bad. This is not a censor and this is not a feeling that the idea has to be complete or perfect; it just has

---

[7]Times are indicative and are best 'improvised' as you see the group write.

to have 'legs' – potential to create more ideas, characters and situations to make the idea theatrical.

Writing exercise: Guided imagery

Now repeat the exercise but this time I will begin with an image – a literal image, such as a photograph or a painting.

It may be an artwork that implies or suggests interesting or problematic situations and/or relationships. You then need to provide the given circumstances or information to make sense of the image. Who is this? Where are they? Why? Who else lives here? etc.

Begin writing an internal monologue from the perspective of someone in the scene.

Or you can write a scene inspired by that image. Don't be bound by trying to write in a linear fashion – perhaps experiment writing an episodic structure or write ritualistically/surreal images/symbols. They don't need to follow on, or even make sense at this point.

I will be introducing ideas and images that will encourage a more stylized, surreal scene.

For example:

- At four minutes – the character holds a glass, empty but cracked.
- At six minutes – they feel something in their pocket and find a single key.
- At eight minutes – the sound of a water fall drowns out their conversation.
- At twelve minutes – car headlights blind them.
- At sixteen minutes – blue light floods the scene.
- At eighteen minutes – a siren deafens them.
- At twenty minutes, the smell of burnt toast distracts them.
- At twenty-two minutes – find an end.
- At twenty-five minutes – finish.

Now repeat the process of looking for gold.

Writing exercise: Guess my play

(N. B. This activity only works once with a cohort but demonstrates the way creative ideas can be generated through simple scaffolds.)

Tell the student(s) that you have a great idea for a play and they can have it if they guess it. Students make suggestions such as 'Is it about a police officer?' The truth is, you don't have an 'idea' – but will answer yes or no to their question based on an arbitrary system. I often would just say 'yes' to questions that ended in a vowel and no to questions ending with a consonant.

The 'yes' ideas are written on the board. Each new random piece of information generates new ideas from the students and they 'make sense' of these facts as if they were intentionally chosen.

Needless to say a play emerges from nothing.

Only after the exercise do you mention how the ideas were chosen to emphasize that it is not the quality of the ideas but what you do with them that makes a play emerge.

Writing exercise: Character A and Character B

Write a scene with two unnamed characters, Character A and Character B.

Character A wants something from Character B; it can be an actual item like money or an emotion like trust or an action like an apology.

However, Character B has a really good reason for not being willing (or able) to provide it.

Write three to four pages. Make sure you clearly end the scene. Alternatively, use this as a workshop improvisation and record the interaction. Transcribe the scene and look for ideas, dialogue or character that could be developed further.

Writing exercise

Version 1: Whole class free writing and improvisation

Using index cards or post-it notes, write down as many ideas as you can, one idea per note, for each of the following:

- Topics you care about.
- Characters who would be interesting to meet.
- Characters you would hate to meet.
- Places where there is potential for tension.
- Situations you hate being in.

Stick these on a wall/whiteboard in 'like' groups – all the characters together, all the themes together, etc.

Now, do something else – in a classroom you could do some quick improvisation exercises to get you out of your heads.

If you are working alone, get up and do something physical – a walk or a run, or even some housework.

Then, after letting the ideas incubate, return to the lists.

Choose two character post-its and one note from each of the other sections.

This is a quick random activity; let the combination of ideas generate the situation and action – don't try to find combinations that will work.

Decide what the characters want from each other or from the situation. What is their relationship? Status?

Then increase the stakes. Ask, 'What if?' questions. Imagine what would happen if one of the character's reputation/job/relationship/life depended on the outcome of the meeting.

Choose a situation that has the most theatrical potential and begin to write.

Version 2: Improvised collaborative playwriting

Think of as many characters, places, actions as you can.

Write each one on a separate card.

Create three piles – character cards, action cards, place cards.

Shuffle the cards.

In pairs or groups of three, collect a character card each and one from the other two piles for each pair/group.

Think of a situation that these ideas suggest and improvise a scene.

Reflect on the good bits from the scene. What worked? What was interesting?

Redo the scene, developing the ideas that worked.

Now perform the prepared scenes in front of the class and I will debrief and guide class discussion of the gold in each scene.

The 'gold' is then taken away to be the beginning or a group written scene.

In your groups, choose a moment (shown in tableaux/ statues) that demonstrates what the problem is at the beginning of the scene. Then choose two more moments and tableaux – a moment from the middle that showed the struggle and then one from the end that showed the conclusion.

Form the opening tableau and, after justifying the physical positions improvise until you get to the second moment, then justify and get to the third.

Write the dialogue (and the stage directions) to form the group written scene.

The scene you write is the first draft; it is not meant to be the finished play. The idea is to write something that will allow you to develop character, situation or concept.

How good is the idea?
Evaluating creativity

Evaluation at the right time is a major aspect of creativity (Bailin, 2011).

A student's work will be assessed by how well it achieves its objectives and how well it follows its own rules. This is the play's coherence or how well it succeeds in its intention.

Some ideas to consider when evaluating student work are the following:

- Is the idea authentic and true to the voice of the student?
- Is the world created for the play clear and sustained?
- Does it follow and obey its own rules?
- Can the world be visualized on stage?
- How has the idea, the theme or concern been transformed into a theatrical vehicle/situation/character?
- Is the vehicle
  - a character? A central protagonist who drives the action?
  - a story? An analogy?
  - a plot structure such as an epic narrative with an Ibsenesque back story that causes all the complications in the present – for example, *Ghosts*?
  - in the language? Is it in a symbol or a motif?
- On what journey does this vehicle take the audience?

The key questions are the following: What do you want the audience to experience in the theatre of your play? What do you want them to feel, think, when they leave your play?

The objective can be open – it need not be didactic. Simon Stephens suggests that the only questions worth asking are the ones you don't know the answers to – they may want the audience to question or to act. While Brecht had a definite objective, and his politics were pretty clear, student playwrights need not be afraid of a range of possible responses. The tension is that a play is a conversation – a dialogue with the ideas and the audience.

The journey for the audience will require a specific kind of journey for the play and that in turn suggests a kind of journey for the characters. What is important is that the ideas are hidden in this vehicle or in the characters' words and behaviours – a play is about an audience's discovery.

The idea needs to unfold for an audience and emerge in a way that sustains engagement and, perhaps, offers the opportunity for multiple responses.

Summary

- Idea generation deserves pedagogical attention. Teaching and learning strategies that address idea generation and development will help students begin well.
- Focusing on what kind of play and what kind of theatrical experience the student wants to create for an audience keep the idea theatrical and embodied – rather than literary and theoretical.
- Focusing on the play as performance will ensure the work on idea generation is effective and efficient.
- By clarifying what students believe you can clarify what students want to say, question or discuss.
- Focusing on strong beliefs will keep the stakes high and give the students scope to find their voice.
- They may write about their lives but will need to find a dramatic and theoretical distancing device to keep it engaging for an audience.

- Writing a premise or statement of purpose will clarify the objective for the playwright and give them a destination for their thinking, research and pre-writing.

- Concepts, position and opinions will remain theatrical if they are linked to a metaphor or image early in the development.

- Finding a vehicle for the idea will help them turn their concepts into situations.

- Students can use a variety of writing exercises to find the idea and develop their understanding of their vision or concept.

- The creative process involves alternating between free imaginative writing and creative evaluation of ideas.

References

Bailin, S. (2011). 'Creativity and Drama Education'. In S. Schonmann (Ed.), *Key Concepts in Theatre/Drama Education* (pp. 209–13). Rotterdam: Sense Publications.

Catron, L. E. (2002). *The Elements of Playwriting*. Long Grove, IL: Waveland Press, Inc.

Egri, L. (1960). *The Art of Dramatic Writing*. New York: Simon and Schuster.

Freeman, J. (2016). *New Performance/New Writing* London: Palgrave Macmillan.

Gooch, S. (2001). *Writing a Play*. London: A & C Black.

Herrington, J. and Brian, C. (Eds). (2006). *Playwrights Teach Playwriting: Revealing Essays by Contemporary Playwrights*. Hanover, NH: Smith and Kraus.

Itallie, J.-C. v. (1997). *The Playwright's Workbook*. Montclair, NJ: Applause Theatre and Cinema Books.

Jester, C. and Stoneman, C. (2012). *Playwriting Across the Curriculum*. London and New York: Routledge.

Spencer, S. (2002). *The Playwright's Guidebook*. London: Faber and Faber.

Stephens, S. (2016). *Simon Stephens: A Working Diary*. London and New York: Bloomsbury Methuen Drama.

Taylor, V. (2002). *Stage Writing*. Ramsbury (England): Crowood Press.

Wesker, A. (2010). *Wesker on Theatre*. London: Oberon Books.

7

Creating character

So, I think, fundamentally, 'Who are my characters?
What do they want? What's stopping them from getting
what they want? What have they done in order to get it?
And from that build a narrative.

SIMON STEPHENS

Introduction

The last chapter looked at the students' ideas and explored
how they can transform opinions into concepts and then to a
theatrical vision.

This chapter explores how to create characters as vehicles
for the developing theatrical vision.

Alternatively, if you have a student more interested in
'people' than ideas, the activities in this chapter can also be
used as the starting point of the writing process to generate a
theatrical vision.

Ideas and characters

The relationship between idea and character is an important
one for students and teachers to understand.

Students (and all of us) create our understanding of the world through our experience of it. If we see the world as a safe and happy place, that is because of the experiences we have had and how we have responded to them. If we see the world as competitive and unforgiving, it is because of what has happened to us and how we have reacted. If we see the world as unstable and violent it is because of the life we have lived. These reactions are also impacted by our particular sensibilities. Many young people watch the violence and corruption in the news without feeling anything while others find it distressing and become anxious and disillusioned.

Students' conclusions and ideas about the world have come from making sense of these experiences. And these experiences have involved people. It is their reflections on observing real people 'act' in their world that has led to their conclusions/ opinions. It is their interactions with people and their behaviour – in their home, in their communities and in their world – that has taught them what it means to be 'human'. After viewing people act they have turned these observations into conclusions, positions and concepts – jealousy makes people bitter or kindness heals (most) hurts.

To write a play, students return these abstract ideas back to the world of people through creating characters – unreal, composite and representative, but people nonetheless.

Then they place those people in situations of conflict.

So, to make the concept specific, playwrights create characters to live in their world and live the reality of the idea – loneliness, betrayal or racism. A character is placed in situations where they experience events or relationships that bring cruelty or joy, or live the mundane reality of betrayal or success. These imagined lives help students articulate and understand what they believe and discover the questions they want to ask or discuss.

Students would often come to me at the beginning of the process with an idea for a play and I would (partially) jokingly ask: 'Great, but who is in it and what do they want?'

So, if a student has completed the tasks from last chapter they will have created several situations in which to explore their play's central idea. They now need to create/develop the characters who will struggle in these situations. And in dramatic works, these characters need depth and specificity.

Writing exercise: Visualize your characters

One of the ways to keep a scene visual is to remember that you are writing about people who will move about in space and that you are asking the characters to interact as well as speak. Maria Irene Fornes (in Svich, 2009) encourages the use of daydreaming to activate the visual imagination.

This exercise asks you to visualize your character.

Think about a character in your play and imagine what they look like.

Let yourself daydream about them in the *location* of the scene.

(Try at this stage to imagine the location as a real place – not as a stage set.)

Focus on what you can see, that is, only what an audience would be able to 'read'.

Now sketch your character in as much detail as you can. This is to give you an image of what presence you want them to have in the scene. (Don't worry too much about the background or your drawing ability.)

Now, unpack this – write a description of what the audience will see as the character enters.[1] How do they move? Are they confident, nervous, commanding?

Note any physical qualities that reveal or impact on character. Are they tall? Messy in the way they dress?

---

[1]Adapted from Itallie (1997).

Think of qualities that are out of their control such as their age or height or that they are losing their hair.

Then think of things that they have chosen – Is their hair dyed? Are they wearing very expensive clothes? – anything that would reveal something about themselves and that would impact on how other characters see them. Think of whether they have cultivated this image – expensive clothes – and whether it is true or a performance/mask.

Then ask: Are they successful in their choices? Is their hair piece obvious or their fake tan too orange(!).

Consider a piece of jewellery, a jacket, a watch that could be symbolic – a gift, an heirloom, a prop to show wealth – or a sign of how tough their life has been – a scar, perhaps.

These are aimed at generating ideas about character and you certainly do not need to give every character all of these. But it focuses you on communicating something about your character visually – showing not telling.

The audience reads everything for meaning. If it is there, it will be seen as important. Use this to your advantage.

Writing characters and autobiography

As discussed in the last chapter, young people (and to some extent all writers) often mine their own lives for inspiration when creating character. The plays your students write will be populated with personalities and characters which, to a certain degree, will be cobbled together from the people in their lives.

A character is constructed through a process of collecting bits and pieces from the people in their world and rearranging them to create new people.

The conclusions from my research also suggest that a student will write about themselves. As with their idea, the impact of autobiographical content – even that disguised through metaphor – is worthy of discussion. Arthur Miller reports in his memoir that, while not realizing it fully at the time, Willy

Loman's feelings of self-doubt and uncertainty accurately reflected his own feelings about himself then and throughout his life (1995, p. 69). The students in my research wrote about the experiences that affected them the most – moments of turmoil or disillusionment. As discussed, this can be liberating and empowering if they employ a theatrical distancing device and character can create that distance.

But, as Simon Stephen (2016) warns, the creative urge is not therapy. Aspects of a writer's personality may bleed into their characters – but it is not the objective. As students need to focus on creating characters in action, biography as source material may be counterproductive, as it often encourages a retell – a passive story of events that happened to people.

Creating an artistic vehicle is very important. Remind your students that they will always be focusing their characterization on furthering the central idea: Characters serve the play, not reality. The character can be *like* the person they know – they cannot *be* the person they know.

How do we know character?

To understand a character an audience pays attention to the following:

- what they say,
- what is said to them,
- what is said about them(especially when they are not in the room) and
- what the character does – how they treat others, whether they keep their promises and, overall, whether their behaviour matches their words (and if it doesn't, an audience will believe their actions).

In creating character, a playwright needs to manage all these sources of information.

Edgar (2009, p. 47) suggests that the character is only known through this matrix of impressions presented to the audience by the playwright – there is no real character beyond the text. An audience understands a character through what they do – their actions – as they reveal what they want and therefore who they are. (Action is dealt with more fully in the next chapter.)

When creating character, a playwright needs to understand a character well enough to know how they will react or what choices they will make. A playwright needs to know what their characters think and feel – what their strengths are and what makes them fearful – to understand what they will choose when faced with a complication. The play moves forward by the choices the characters make and the consequences that result. And, as Tidmarsh (2014, p. 15) suggests, audience engagement is increased when those choices are *active*.

While you want to write characters that the audience will see as consistent, the playwright needs to navigate the line between surprising the audience with unexpected actions and yet creating believable responses appropriate to the world of the play.

Considering the complexity of a character's hierarchy of wants, contradictions are inevitable – they just need to be believable within the world created by the writer.

To understand the character they create, playwrights often write detailed character studies or profiles to ensure they are rounded, complex and consistent. Neipris (2005) suggests that you need to know all that you can about your characters and draw up elaborate biographies that explore the intricacies of each character's past. In this approach, the more the playwright knows a character the more they will be able to know what they *would* (might) do in any situation.

Creating complex character detail allows the writer to let the characters 'loose' within the confines of the play. They are free to act and counteract, based upon the parameters of their personality, background and beliefs. This interaction can give the impression of characters taking over – the cliché of them 'writing the play'. But, as Wandor (2008) argued, this is more correctly just the combination of two or more realistic characters who collaborate and interact, so the new ideas are a product of combinations of actions, reactions and responses.

The other benefit of writing detailed backgrounds is that it allows the writer to understand the actions of the characters – both their noble and base desires. Creating a 'back story' will allow the writer to understand their characters – especially important for the 'antagonists' or villains – so we know why they are the way they are. For each character, I ask my students to consider: 'What has happened to them?' This asks what events – traumas, challenges, triumphs – have formed the character's view of the world. However, it is best for writers to be flexible, recognizing the balance between writing backgrounds before they start and knowing that characters will unfold in the action of the play.

Complexity and contradictions are necessary in these characters to increase the stakes and to make the struggle real. Life is messy and so are plays.

Wright (1997, p. 18) suggests that writing monologues or out-scenes is a great way to create specific details about characters. Writing dialogue that does not/will not exist in the play encourages the writer to explore the backgrounds of their characters using theatrical processes and discovering theatrical solutions. In this approach, the best way to understand or create a character's relationship with, say, their parent is to write a scene that explores a key moment in their history: the neglected birthday or the missed school presentation, or the time the worried parent waited up for the child who had missed curfew. The benefit is that the student practices *the voice* of each character as they explore the events and experiences that have 'created' them. Wright argues that this encourages the writer to take on the perspective of the character in their world (1997, p. 23). Another option is to explore the characters at crucial moment in their lives. Wright (1997) suggests writing duologue scenes where characters work through problematic, traumatic or defining moments in their lives through confiding in a friend or trusted 'advisor'.

Deciding who the character would or could tell and which events and which moments were significant to them reveal/ generate much about the character.

Writing exercise: The monologue

Maria Irena Fornes (in Svich, 2009) encourages playwrights to use monologues to explore your character's emotional memory.

Writing monologues from different times in the character's life encourages the writer to imagine the life journey of the character to explore what and who made them who they are. These monologues, from different stages in their identity development, should explore the feelings, ambitions and fears at *that* time. What they choose to talk about is what is most important.

Say your character is twenty-five years old.

Write a monologue from the perspective of your character at twelve years old.

What was vital to them at that time? Write their thoughts on an event or an interaction, or a problem or realization.

This is not a retelling from the adult perspective 'remembering' how they once felt; it is an immediate reaction/ reflection by them at the time just after, that night, the next day.

Now write another monologue for your character at sixteen (or an appropriately significant age), then another at twenty-one, then twenty-five – that is their age in the play.

How has their perspective changed? What has happened in their life to change their world view, personality, etc.

If the character is older, choose four relatively equidistant ages – 12, 20, 28, 36, or 12 , 24, 36, 48, etc.

Writing monologues is an effective way to create/understand the character, allowing you to walk in their shoes, allowing the character to (apparently) reveal themselves. Through creating life experiences, you generate answers to your 'who am I' and 'why am I' questions for your character.

Building character profiles

A more conventional approach – and one that works for actors as much as writers – is for the writer to create a back story for the character through answering questions and compiling lists. That is, once the broad characteristics have been established (age, profession and relationship to other characters, say), some writers encourage explicit unpacking of these generalities by imagining and creating specific details.

This approach to character is based on the tropes of realistic acting methods, where actors use or imagine detailed backstory information to understand their character's motivations so their performances will be 'alive' (Moore, 1991). Just as an actor prepares a role by understanding given circumstances, the playwright enriches their play be 'writing for' this dimension, creating both possibilities for the actor to find and a richness to inspire a director.

Writing exercise: Character background 1

To explore, develop and understand characters and their overarching objective, many writers carry out extensive preparatory work. This work begins with imaginary or creative exercises.

To know a character and how they will behave, you can create a 'world' for your character by considering the following interrelated aspects. In your writer's journal, make extensive notes under the following questions using the included sub-questions as a guide.

1. *Background*

Where did they come from?

What their life was like up until the start of the scene/play will be affected by where they live, who they live with, what life/world events have impacted them and the people around them and will affect the way people react to them – status/class/education as well as accent/dialect.

2. *Beliefs*

What they believe/feel/think/know?

This explores how their views motivate and propel the characters in the play. What they do comes from what they believe because that is what they fight for. What Spencer (2002) calls attitudes. It is their world view.

3. *Baggage*

What has happened to them?

These are the experiences that have contributed to the beliefs and motivations. It focuses on those aspects of character which are the product of our experiences, context and genetics.

What trauma, challenges or triumphs have they experienced?

Emotional baggage is a rich source of internal conflict and often a product of the specifics of their background. For example, an only child who was spoilt or neglected might take this into adulthood.

Was the character affected by tragedy early in life? Recently?

What kind of life did they lead? A working-class character who was abused by their own class or who suffered brutality in their environment will see the world differently to one who was insulted or humiliated by the upper class.

These ideas generate specific details and stop a writer reproducing clichéd generalizations about backgrounds or experiences.

Creating your characters

In realist and/or conventional plays, there is a central protagonist whose objectives – wants – are incompatible with those of an equally determined antagonist. Conflict arises when the antagonist confronts the protagonist. Characters in a closed text like this are predictable and 'knowable' and will behave in consistent though complex ways. They live in a world where individuals are agents operating with free will and there is a cause-and-effect relationship between what a character does and the outcome of the play.

In these plays, the playwright creates an overarching objective for their characters. As discussed in Chapter 6, all plays need to have an overall objective and this can be tied to the journey of the central protagonist. Even in ensemble plays – where the 'Whose play is it?' question is not as clear cut or appropriate – each character will have an overarching objective. The mix of objectives creates the dramatic tension and suspense that drives the piece and keeps the audience engaged.

Characters and wants

Most dramatic works are still about people and what they want and how desperate they are to achieve it.

This section explores character in the context of writing plays about *people* in conflict. While I will consider less realist figures and roles later, realistic character is an effective starting point for young people learning how to write a play.

A play is about people (or representations of people, for example, puppets) striving to achieve their objectives and trying to get what they want. Every action – speaking and physical behaviour – is made to achieve something.

For students writing a short play, choosing to create a central protagonist can help bring their idea into focus – on one person in one situation who, through complications, changes and/or grows through the journey of the play.

To write engaging characters for a realistic play, students will need to know what these characters want – from life, from the situation of the play, and from the other characters they encounter. A playwright creates and understands the details of their imagined individuals, so they can predict how they will react and respond in relationship to other characters and changing situations.

Further, what a character wants needs to be significant; there needs to be something at stake. To paraphrase Dorothy Heathcote, we go to a play to see people in a mess. These stakes need to be heightened throughout the course of the play, so the character needs to become more desperate or more determined, more in love or more embittered. Characters reveal themselves in moments of crisis where their mettle is proven or dissolved. The higher the stakes, the more prepared the audience will be to accept extreme behaviour.

As Edgar (2009, p. 51) suggests, because we find characters in extreme situations and exceptional circumstances, we find them behaving uncharacteristically. This allows for playwrights to embrace contradictions that may be lurking just inches below the character's surface.

Understanding wants

To explore the complexity and potential for contradictions within a character consider three aspects of wants.

Hierarchy

Characters want more than one thing. And they always want some things more than others.[2] The potential for conflict or

---

[2] I consciously don't consider needs here – because I want to explore character choices – and when a 'need' like sleep is forgone for a want – approval – then it is the choice that is interesting.

complications in your play is increased by creating characters with internal contradictions. Individuals with complicated internal conflicts and contradictions contribute greatly to audience engagement. An individual's ability to navigate and manage their conflicting wants is often difficult and therefore dramatic.

Organizing the characters wants into what Rivera (cited in Herrington and Brian, 2006) calls a *hierarchy* allows you to identify/create areas for potential conflict within and around the character – that is, inner and external obstacles.

These contradictions may be incidental, adding colour to the character, e.g. a health fanatic who loves bacon. Or they can be *essential* to the conflict and complications that drive the play. An example (borrowed from recent political history) *could* revolve around a high-profile powerful political figure (a president or the like) who jeopardizes his want to maintain his position, and the power, respect and prestige that goes with it, because he wants the romantic attention of a young intern. These dilemmas and the opportunities they create for betrayal, deception and moments of intense conflict are exciting to watch.

This conflict of wants prompts dramatic questions for the audience: Did the internal conflict cause a momentary reordering of his wants, only to be changed back once the events became 'public'? Would he have lied if he knew he would get caught? (Consider how less dramatic it would be if he just eloped with the intern!)

This emphasizes for students the potential for internal conflict to create drama, and on its ability to act as a catalyst for further complications, especially as it reveals weaknesses that empower external obstacles – 'protagonists' included (see Chapters 8 and 10).

Conscious or unconscious?

Another aspect of wants is the possibility that characters may not actually be conscious or completely aware of the objectives or wants that motivate them – until or even after they surface.

As Sweet (1993) suggests, this lack of self-knowledge results in people seeming to act irrationally, until it is revealed that unconscious wants were motivating their actions. For example, a central internal, and subsequent external, conflict faced by Arthur Miller's Eddie Carbone in *A View from the Bridge* is his complicated feelings for his niece. While troubled by Catherine's 'growing up' and her involvement with her boyfriend Rodolpho, Eddie is not aware of all the reasons for his 'overprotective' concern for her until it is too late and the stakes become too high. To destroy their relationship, he humiliates everyone – including himself – by acting out of character and kissing Rodolpho. This action creates further conflict, further actions, and Eddy's denial of his feelings drives the subsequent tragedy.

Consciously or not, characters often don't say what they want. Simon Stephens suggests that characters never say what they really want. Unconscious motivation presumes characters are based on real people. Yet, stylized characterization can explore and exploit the theatricality and symbolic potential of these unconscious and contradictory wants or traits. Think of Brecht's MacHeath with his white gloves or Il Capitano's traditionally threadbare waistcoat under his military coat.

In *The Threepenny Opera*, Brecht symbolizes the aspirations of his central character, the mobster MacHeath, with the upper-class white gloves that cover the blood-stained hands underneath. The conflicting objectives – wealth and power at all cost versus respectability – are emblemized in this gesture. Similarly, Il Capitano, the mercenary, brags about his bravery and military exploits – though his real poverty, symbolized by the condition of his undergarments, reflects the conflicting wants. He wants to be respected and treated as a hero, but his desire not to come to any harm (in other words his cowardice) has meant that his successes, and therefore payment, have been minimal.

As we see, all is not what it seems and writers can decide how much the character is aware of their own contradictions.

Masks

Thinking of character as *mask* – both in a psychological and theatrical sense – explores an approach to characterization that reminds us that all identity is a performance.

It considers the extent to which a person's multiple and possibly contradictory wants are impacted by context. Related to hierarchy, it understands the differing faces we present to different people and the masks we adopt in different contexts and situations.

It plays with the fluidity of identity and challenges the expectation of predictable and consistent characters. People adopt roles to achieve what they want, what Edgar (2009) calls *characters* acting. In this sense we see *character* as an action to get what you want.

The multiple masks are also a good source of conflict in a more conventional approach. The different masks we adopt for different contexts may be incompatible. Your character may be both a daughter and a successful executive – the doting child mask needs to stay separate from the ruthless company CEO or they will destroy each other. While conflicting wants can create different masks, the same want – acceptance, success, pleasure – in a different context may require different masks.

Character as mask opens a playwright to a metaphorical treatment of character. The persona adopted by each character, willingly or unconsciously and in each context, allows a more symbolic and analogous exploration of the play's ideas and relationships. Characters *may only* be a mask – a figure, a type, a position – and this can mean playwrights can concentrate and reduce breadth of character for precision to convey the idea of the play. It explores the poetic dimension that Hall encourages: emblematic characters and figure. Like the roles of Chaplain and Cook in Brecht's *Mother Courage and Her Children*, there need not be a rounded character underneath the mask. They exist to fulfil a role.

Wants as symbols of character

What a character wants both reflects and creates character. A character's immediate wants can be symbolic or emblematic of their super-objective. A want is expressed in action but what that action is, and what it may do to others, adds further to our understanding of the character and the play. Therefore, what a character wants – to be powerful and respected – tells us about them, but how they go about achieving this – through hard work and generosity or through blackmail and illicit favours – reveals just as much about the character. Eddie Carbone in Miller's *A View from the Bridge* was willing to die rather than face, personally or publicly, the truth of his unconscious desires.

Wants can also emblemize the character. They reveal not only contradictions but the *poetry* of the stage persona.

In Polly Stenham's *That Face* the characters' wants are complex and twisted. Martha's specific wants in the final scene – for Henry to drink with her and to dress like her – reveals Martha's desire for him to be complicit in her fantasy. Yet Henry's acquiescence, his want to appease her, at first symbolizes love, but quickly becomes emblematic of his co-dependency – symbolized by him wearing her clothes. It reveals that he is invested in this dysfunctional dynamic as much as Martha.

So, we can ask what the character wants and explore if these objectives reveal or emblemize their character.

Through choosing the specific actions aimed at achieving their wants, a playwright can create poetry, symbol, motif and character signs that affect an audience in a theatrical way. Like Martha, a character who wants to be *served* a drink all the time may want to be looked after or treated as important. Are they seeking comfort in the alcohol or the company? Are they removing the guilt by rationalizing the action – a constant party stops you confronting the reality of being an alcoholic. Consider how character is affected by a want to serve others alcohol all the time. This reinforces the interconnection of action, character and symbol.

Writing exercise: Realist approach to your character's backstory

Here are two approaches to creating a background for your character.

Approach 1

The first consists of a series of questions and answers that generate details about the character that will affect their behaviour in the play.

These details create, explain and explore character motivations become the source of the conflict that generates the action of the play.

This is a list of questions adapted from a Stanislavsky-inspired realist acting process used by actors to prepare for a role. They help an actor create rich details to build characters they can 'inhabit' (Moore, 1991).

This information is only important if it helps you understand how the character will react, interact and respond to others and events.

Questions

1. Who am I?

Write their full name and age.

Who is in their family?

How do they feel about their family?

Describe their relationship with their parents: their siblings; their extended family – uncles, aunts, grandparents and others.

What did (or will) make them move out of home?

What is their favourite place to go?

Who do they call when they are in trouble?

What item do they have on them right now that reveals character? (Medication/cigarette lighter/someone else's phone.)

Describe their last day of school.

What is their greatest fear?

What is their darkest secret?

What is their most precious memory?

What is the best and worst thing that could happen to them?

What are ten things no one knows about them?

2. *Where do they live?*

Their home? Their street? Their town/city?

What country are they in?

Where are they at the beginning of the play?

What is their 'world'? Who else lives there?

This focus on location is about context. Also consider their relationship to the environment:

Are they indoors or outdoors (either 'imagine' or is it given)?

Where are they most at home? Where do they feel the most comfortable?

What effect does the environment have on them? Does this make them cold/happy/depressed?

Are they comfortable with the luxury/instability/hostility? Remember Shakespeare's use of weather to foreshadow disaster.

These decisions are all meant to increase the stakes and make things more difficult for the character.

3. *When is it?*

What time in 'history' is it? What are the events that surround them?

This helps place the character in a social time. If they haven't considered this, it may be a way to increase the universality of the ideas in their play. What would happen if we set the play in another time?

What time of day? What does that mean for how they feel/
interact? Are they a late-night person? Early morning?
Keep this in mind when you write your scenes and the time they
are set. (This also generates further details for the situation.)

For example, scene two of Polly Stenham's *That Face*
begins in the morning after the night before. The events of the
previous night put emotional stress and the 'early' morning
places physical stress on the characters.

4. *What do they want?*

This is the basis of the character's action – and this question
needs to be answered in a complex, detailed way:

- Life objective – what this character wants out of
  the entire journey of their life – what is their ultimate
  goal?
- Main objective – what do they want by the end of the
  play? At the end of the scene?
- Immediate objective – what do they want right
  now? This can change a few times, even in short scenes.
- What else do they want? Think contradictory objectives
  and a hierarchy of wants.

5. *Why do they want it and how far are they willing to go to get it?*

Remember the greater the stakes the more an audience is
engaged unless it becomes melodramatic.

The 'why' or motivation can be found in their back story
and the impact of past decisions or past experiences. This also
incorporates unconscious motivations.

For example, an early experience of death for a character
could create a fear of abandonment and result in an adult
who is either overly clingy or one so guarded they don't let
people in.

The reasons for wants may actually contradict their stated
public persona – career ambition might be motivated by

resentment rather than self actualization. This heightens the stakes and creates a sense of ambiguity and contradiction.

6. *How are they going to achieve it?*

This is the range of actions, physical and emotional, they are willing to undertake to satisfy their wants and overcome their obstacles. These, again, need to be high stakes and, perhaps, even life and death (even if it's a metaphorical death, such as career suicide or loss of family/home life). This is the action of the play. The more extreme the range of actions, the more likely the play will shock an audience – if that is the playwright's goal.

7. *What is stopping them? What is against them?*

These can be internal obstacles – failings (greed, lust and/or anger) or weaknesses (self-esteem, anxiety or illness) or a combination of both. Obstacles clearly include contradictory goals and the struggle to achieve all of them. This also includes the decisions regarding which ones are more important or more likely to keep them happy.

Obstacles are also external – a rival (the traditional antagonist) or even a character that keeps them from full awareness, an overbearing parent, partner or peer, or a system (class/racism/bigotry, etc.). External obstacles include poverty, isolation, environment, class, etc. This is the conflict of the play.

Work through these questions answering them in free-flowing prose. The level of detail required here depends on the style, size and form of the piece. A short one-act play needs much less detail than a full length play.

Then put them away for a day, or a week. After that, go back and see what they tell you about the person and how that might impact on the other person/people in the scene.

Repeat the process for all the characters in your play.

Writing exercise: Symbols of character – the backpack

When I teach characterization to secondary drama students I use a handbag/backpack activity.

To demonstrate that they understand a character in a published script or that they 'know' the character they are creating, I ask them to create a virtual backpack – using images – that includes emblematic or symbolic objects and possessions to reflect and/or create character. (In the days before digital culture students would create an old-fashioned collage from magazines!)

The objective is for the students to imagine what items would show the various and conflicting aspects of character. Sometimes they are obvious, like a phone or packet of gum, but students are encouraged to encapsulate and reveal the contradictions and inner turmoil: contraception in the handbag of a devout Catholic, betting receipts and overdue bills, prescriptions for medication for a life-threatening disease, uncashed cheques, cigarette lighter and asthma medication, crucifix, eviction notice, bank statement showing $7.90, etc.

But playwriting isn't psychology, it's theatre

The value of background work is that it creates the detail necessary for the student to write their play. Rounded characters only need to be coherent in their world. As Tidmarsh (2014, p. 7) suggests, too much character work, backgrounds and contextualizing can lead to static characters, forgetting that everyone – not just the protagonist – will change and grow during the course of the play.

Another aspect to consider is the notion of being able to 'know' a character. All characters – realistic or stylized – are artifice and are created by a writer to pursue their objectives to explore ideas. Gooch (2001) challenges Stanislavskiesque realism by suggesting that, as characters aren't real, there is no real 'breadth' to know beyond the details in the text. Creating details of a character's background is a tool. It can be done, but in the understanding that we do not know the background of people in our lives and yet can read and understand them enough to communicate and form relationships.

And, like the real masks we wear to navigate society, I suggest that we can't *really* know people in life so we shouldn't expect to know everything about the characters in our play. The contradictions and artifice of everyday interaction is even more heightened on the stage.

Freud would even say we don't really know ourselves completely. A character can be created but with missing parts and contradictions. We know that the audience will fill in the blanks for the character in the way we fill in the blanks for the people we know and meet in life. Therefore, writing characters with some blanks to be filled allows an active role for the audience.

Physical approaches to character

For the first part of this chapter I have explored realistic people in realistic plays – characters with a psychological 'truth'. Thus, the internal life of the character created their external presence in the play – what they wanted, why they wanted it, etc. – an 'inside-out' approach.

This section explores less naturalistic or non-psychological-based approaches to character creation. It encourages an 'outside-in' approach to character using physicality and 'energy' to create characters. For this reason, this approach and the activities work particularly well in a classroom situation. They allow whole class drama-based workshop activities to precede, inform and activate writing work. Embodied and experiential teaching and learning strategies, while reminding students they are writing for a future live event, also take advantage of the positive and inclusive strategies that increase student engagement and creativity.

These activities can be introductory work for realistic characters, but they allow students to create character 'figures' that fulfil roles in their plays that are stylized and theatrical. The physical characters may be what they need – energy and roles – not people as such.

Post-dramatic theatre

Reflecting the spectrum of open or closed texts as explored in Chapter 4, this section highlights how non- or post-dramatic approaches to theatre can enliven writing for the stage and discusses the use of roles and 'figure conceptions' to create dramatic and non-dramatic theatre. The world and character types young people create will have a varying proximity or relationship to the world we know. And post-dramatic theatre has encouraged them to imagine worlds that need not be real or even recognizable.

However, despite the developments in post-dramatic theatre that challenge the role of character, most theatre still requires some form of human entity – something that stands for a person. While there are structural and stylistic movements that reject linear and even narrative coherence there are still 'people' in some form or another.

But as all characters are an artifice, the lessons from post-dramatic theatre encourage young people to play around with what a character is and what they 'do' and the *degrees* to which writers need to create coherent and/or consistent characters.

For example, Martin Crimp's *Attempts on Her Life* presents an anti-character, the absent and contradictory character, and asks the audience to make sense of the person who they never meet. Creating a character in their absence, emphasizing contradictions and multiple perspectives, places the audience in the position of bringing meaning to the fragments. This fragmentation offers scope to create dramatic and poetic theatre that evokes experience with, and parallel to, a character journey.

Creating characters from 'energy'

The work of devising companies and the practices of groups inspired by, for example, Jacques Le Coq, demonstrate how physical approaches to character can help writers create theatrical characters.

Playing with physical approaches to character focuses the writer on the different kinds of energy characters bring to the scene.

The workshop approaches to writing/devising below can help writers convey their ideas through physicality, before or instead of text. They play with primal and (arguably) universal symbols and signs to evoke theatrical poetry – meaning beyond words.

Writing exercise: Characters from elements

This approach to character creation examines the qualities and dynamics of the elements. It examines what working with the elements will mean for individual characters and the interactions between them.

Phase 1

Consider the four elements: water, fire, earth and air.

Consider each element in turn and improvise the qualities these elements have in terms of energy, rhythm, speed, tone, texture, mood, etc.

For example, move about the space like water.

What kind of water are you? An ocean? A droplet? A river?
How fast are you moving? Are you moving smoothly?
    Rhythmically?
Do you have a fixed point?
Are you heavy or light?

Explore water through all its extremes.

Choose your preferred water state and continue to move about the space.

What kind of person moves like this?

If we call how you are moving now 100 per cent water, turn this movement into a character by making your movements 50 per cent water and 50 per cent human.

Who is this person?

(If you want to use this process to create realistic characters, continue asking key questions to enable students to imagine this character's life, etc.)

Improvise this person exploring and negotiating an unknown environment.

Imagine your character is in a church for the first time.
or
At a party where they don't know anyone.
or
In a crowd on a busy train platform, etc.

Now turn this into a person who is 30 per cent water and 70 per cent human.

Improvise a short mono drama – working in an office/packing for a trip or cooking a meal, etc. – with or without dialogue.

Go to your journals and answer character questions – who am I? name, etc. – to fill out the background a bit.

Now *emblemize* their personality.

Finish these statements to clarify and 'colour' their character:

My preferred drink is...
I wear...
I drive a...?
I live in a...?, etc.

Now repeat for the other elements.

You will now have four characters based on the elements. Either choose your favourite as the central character or imagine all four in a scene together.

Phase 2

In groups of four, combine two or three elements in a scene – 70/30 earth meets 20/80 air and 40/60 water, etc.

Create situations such as a family outing, a car trip, first date and school reunion.

Improvise these situations, recording the interactions to develop into scenes.

Writing exercise: 'Leading with …' – character from body positions

This exercise begins with exploring fundamental body language techniques to create awareness of physical manifestations of character, then extends to play with body movements, then body energy, to create distinct and rich characters. Begin the lesson with a physical warm-up – a chasing, running or tableau-based game.

Phase 1

Walk around the room in a neutral manner.

Let your arms move freely by your sides and become aware of your own physicality. Then slowly drop all 'uniqueness' and begin to walk as a blank canvas – weight evenly distributed, eyes to the horizon and feet hip width apart.

Now, begin to lead with your nose. Push your nose as far forward as possible. Let your nose draw you through space.

What does that do to your body? How does it make you feel? What attitude does it create?

Keep it as extreme as you can.

Now dial it back until its about 50 per cent. Then adjust slightly until it's the 'human' you want to explore.

Continuing to walk around the room, think as your new character and begin an internal monologue.

- Give this character a name. Where do they live? Who else lives there? Where are they going?
- What would they sound like? Imagine their voice. Now, bubbling up from the belly, make a sound as your character. It can be a word, a grunt, a sound of approval or disdain.
- Adopt the voice that comes from this physical position as you continue your internal monologue.

Now run to your journals and write down everything you have discovered – restarting or continuing the internal monologue.

Write with the same energy you had while improvising.

I will rush you a little – giving you a countdown after one or two minutes and letting you know when to finish.

Repeat the exercise now leading with your chin, then your chest, your stomach and then your knees, etc.

There are two options for how you can now use these physicalities.

Option 1: Improvised monologues

You now have a few different characters. Choose the one you like the most and write a monologue. Writing monologues for your characters provides opportunities for other characters to emerge and ideas to be extended that could develop into a play: for example, who they work/live with will become characters in a scene, etc.; what happens to them in their childhood is 'baggage' for their present selves, etc. These monologues could be extreme and perhaps even surreal to correspond to the extreme physicality that created them – still 'people' but perhaps figures or roles rather than characters.

Option 2: Improvised interactions (facilitating paired scene writing)

Students choose their favourite character.

As a class, improvise a cocktail party in character, interacting with the characters created by others.

As this unfolds, I will stop the activity when I see good pairs/threes.

Then, in your groups, improvise a scene.

Set it in a neutral but public space – a hotel lobby, a mall, a school yard, a waiting room, etc.

The focus is on how the different energies and physicalities interact – what possibilities emerge from these clashing or complementary entities.

Each scene will be shown to the class. You will then write up the improvisation and extend/complete it – next lesson/ later today.

(This is a good way to create group written plays.)

Then, write a scene with their character and one or two of the characters they met at the party. Once you chose a character, even if they were suggested by another, and once you rename and develop them, they become your character.

Characters in relationships

As a play requires conflicts and complications, it is the *conflicting* wants of each character that create the play. As Gooch (2001, p. 72) suggests, characters are created in interaction, existing in *response* to the other characters and the situation. Like masks, certain traits or beliefs are only evident in context with other characters. The people in your play will have wants, and their ability to satisfy those wants are dependent on the wants and actions of other characters in the play. As the play proceeds, characters are affected by what others do. Change maintains interest and audience engagement, and the higher the stakes the more invested they are in the outcome.

Status

As characters exist in interaction with each other and their context, understanding the concept of status will help students explore the many factors that impact on how individuals respond to each other and to situations.

As status is a socially conferred 'power', it shifts with context, situation and company.

As a social agreement, it always needs re-asserting or re-affirming. This reminds students that all interactions are potentially problematic and open to conflict.

In relationships, characters will frequently find something to negotiate or wrestle over regarding status and pecking order. It may be a colour to the conflict in a scene or the very heart of the struggle.

Writing with an eye for the status relationships keeps the writer focused on the dramatic – on the actions characters undertake to maintain or better their rank or position.

Two types of status

Who we are as 'character' and 'how' we are as people changes depending on context. We change masks to respond to our differing status in different contexts.

Status in a scene can be explored by examining the interrelationship between its two manifestations – social status and personal status. While often related, exploring the conflict between these two energies can make scenes complex and subtle.

Social status is the amount of power and prestige accorded to the individual by their social position or rank – the level given by their place in society. In simple terms this can be the hierarchy of professions or wealth, of education and class. This is often easy to see and can convey great power in social situations. This kind of status offers great opportunities for conflict/complications and plot points, especially if those with higher status play the 'card', such as the 'don't you know who I am' moment.

Personal status can take two forms. It can refer to the internal integrity of an individual – the principled, secure individual – who has a generous and empathetic approach to life. These qualities may have contributed to their ability to acquire social status but they can be found in any person. This might be described as humility and nobility of character and these people make great friends – dependable, honest and generous. The second form of personal status is morally neutral; it is the charisma or psychological power found in some individuals. This status – either their irresistible attractiveness or coercive skills of manipulation – can give individuals power in a situation that their social position doesn't warrant.

When social status and personal status come into conflict, there are great opportunities for scenes to explore struggle and negotiations.

The difference between actual and perceived status presents another opportunity for playwrights to explore character in relationship. Whether it is caused by a lack of self-awareness or changing context, this tension creates potential conflict – internal and external. For example, as the politician or judge moves further away from their locus of power – from parliament or courtroom to a sporting field, bar or family home – the power of their social status diminishes and perhaps their personal status is revealed.

Other opportunities for status to create conflict arise when there is a disconnect between the internal perception of a character's status and how they are treated – conflict between expectations and reality; for example, the situation of a person who is revered at home and reviled outside. While an obvious rich source of comedy, it could also explore ideas of discrimination based on class, race or religion, and the consequences of these social dissatisfactions for family life. These situations also require decisions regarding the status of all characters, providing scope for defining relationships based on status conflicts.

Status and its impermanence also encourage playwrights to examine how character's change due to the changing context. Exploring how status, personal and social, changes will be real and relevant to young writers, especially as changes to status based on changing currency such as attractiveness, power or intelligence frequently reposition young people in their social hierarchy. Equally, exploring how status diminishes when the conditions that conferred it disappear – youth, beauty, strength, popularity – can drive an entire play. For example, the potential for a person's status to change over time is central to our understanding of *Death of a Salesman*. Willy's inability or unwillingness to accept the changes (or fiction of his status) contributes greatly to the tragedy of the play.

It would also be worth exploring the way status can be conferred on individuals in certain situations that is absent in the rest of their life – the expert in trains or ballroom dancing may only have high status in those specific situations.

Status provides great scope to explore both character depth and potential conflict – internal and external. It also can develop a character's hierarchy of wants – perhaps the train driver is only happy when ballroom dancing – so career success is not really a want. So, offering them a promotion that would impact their 'dance' time would not be an easy decision.

The potential for status to be conveyed through voice and behaviour helps create vibrant theatrical characters. Dialect and word choice can reflect background – geographical and class based – without a character's knowledge or consent. Similarly, class or exposure to wealth can impact on a character's assumptions about the world and allow subtle character information through behaviour (as seen in Marie Antoinette's apocryphal exclamation, 'Let them eat cake'; see Chapter 9).

Writing exercise: Status

Status impacts all interactions.

Part 1

Write a scene set in a department store.
    There are three characters – A, B and C:

- Character A, the customer service person, is new, young and not well educated.
- Character B, a customer, is very well spoken (social status) but petty (personal).
- Character C, another customer, is reserved and highly generous.
- B and C are waiting to be served. A is sorting out items behind the counter.

Improvise or write the scene exploring the *interplay* between the levels of status.
    All characters must be active – they cannot 'give in'. And all have conflicting wants. Work out what they want and see what happens.
    The scene is not to be subtle; play with each character's awareness of self and others, and how this generates or diffuses conflict.
    What happens when characters act to maintain their social status? (Remember, Character A has the most to lose.)
    What happens when they act from high levels of personal status? Where is the conflict?
    Will alliances emerge?

Part 2

Consider a scene you are working on. Consider what changing the status of one of the characters will do to the action of the scene, or the play, and how it may generate further conflicts and complications.

Rewrite the scene so that the status of the characters is used in the conflict. For example, perhaps objectives are thwarted by social status or achieved through personal status. In other words, introduce a fight for status in their fight for their objectives.

Write a new scene for the play where the central characters' personal or social status changes – in this moment, in this situation. They are revealed to be a fraud or a liar or to be weak when they needed to be strong.

The status needs to change because of something that happens: it can be a mistake, an accident or an action that one character does intentionally. The complication can be something that happened a long time ago (e.g. the forgery in *A Doll's House*), just before the scene (*Othello*'s wedding) or as the scene unfolds (*A View from the Bridge*). What does this tell you about the characters?

Part 3

A character's personality (personal status) is revealed in moments of stress.

Choose a character either from your scene or from an earlier exercise.

Improvise or write a short interaction where they are put under some small stress, such as being overlooked for a role in the school play, coming home with a bad haircut, told that their reservation at a restaurant has been cancelled, etc.

How do they react? What does that tell us about the kind of person they are?

Now repeat that same scene, but this time add another character to the scene – their friend, parent, work mate, etc.

What difference does that make to the scene? Does it change the outcome? What does it tell you about your character?

Extension: Perhaps write the scene where they come home to tell a third character about the inconvenience. How truthful are they?

Writing exercise:
Meeting new people

Your character's personality is created in interaction. Understanding how your character behaves when they are put in an uncomfortable situation and/or when they meet new people will give you an insight into their personality and how they treat others.

Activity 1

Choose one of the following situations – birthday party, first day at a new school/job, interschool science/leadership day, jury duty, adult education course, strangers at a mutual friend's wedding.

Write a scene where one of your characters is required to meet a range of new people and introduce themselves.

(Before completing this activity – if you haven't already – read about high-context/low-context dialogue in Chapter 9.)

For example, imagine that one of the characters is very popular at their school and now meets others who are equally high status. Or imagine that your character is overlooked at home and is now actually very well respected in this new situation. Or the school/office bully is now in a situation where they have no power. What do they do? What opportunities for conflict might arise?

For example, write the scene where an office 'bully' is at a workplace convention. How do they respond to new people? What if they meet a bigger bully, or they are disliked?

Activity 2

This activity reminds you to stay focused on action.

Through adapting a workshop improvisation game, you will remember to write for performance, for actors in space and time.

The bench improvisation

Set up a 'park bench' in the workshop space.

Choose two actors – 'A' and 'B'.

'A' sits on the bench.

After 'A' has established themselves, 'B' enters.

Decide a little about the characters before you start – who are they, what is their relationship, where are they – and then imagine a key event/situation that creates a set of objectives: a queue or a waiting room and a reunion or a hotel lobby.

Fight for status.

Initially without words.

What strategies do you use? What happens when you fight too hard?

Then repeat the activity with new actors.

Now allow them to utter one phrase each.

Then repeat once more allowing the actors to play a scene.

Debrief each, and justify and develop the situations that emerged – exploring wants, background, etc. For each situation ask the following questions: Why is this happening? What in the character's past – immediate, mid- or long-term – makes them 'compete' with a stranger? Or are they strangers?

Now, write up these improvised status scenes in your their journal.

As a writing exercise you can be as true to the improvisation as you want or can use that as a starting point.

Perhaps let them interact in stage directions first, then in dialogue.

Who is the other person to them? Do they know each other?

Try to use the same energy and willingness to take risks found in the improvising workshop in your writing. Write an improvised scene – active playwriting is improvisation of the mind.

Summary

- Character and idea are intimately connected.
- Character can begin the writing process or be the vehicle for a developing idea.

- All characters – even the most realistic – are constructs that need to serve the play – not reality.
- While young writers may mine their life for their characters, they still need to be theatrical vehicles for the idea.
- Characters are their actions. They are conveyed and defined by what they want and what they are prepared to do to get it.
- Characters have a hierarchy of often contradictory and sometimes unconscious wants.
- Creating/knowing the backstory of your character can help you understand how they might react to events and interact with other characters.
- But playwriting is about theatre, not psychology. And how well do we know real people anyway?
- Characters can be created from physicality and energy – acting as both characters and as figures and roles.
- Playwrights can create characters through writing monologues and dialogues, visualization and improvisation.

References

Edgar, D. (2009). *How Plays Work*. London: Nick Hern Books.

Gooch, S. (2001). *Writing a Play*. London: A & C Black.

Herrington, J. and Brian, C. (Eds). (2006). *Playwrights Teach Playwriting: Revealing Essays by Contemporary Playwrights*. Hanover, NH: Smith and Kraus.

Itallie, J.-C. v. (1997). *The Playwright's Workbook*. Montclair, NJ: Applause Theatre and Cinema Books.

Miller, A. (1995). *Time Bends*. London: Minerva.

Moore, S. (1991). *Stanislavsky Revealed: The Actor's Guide to Spontaneity on Stage*. New York: Applause Theatre Books.

Neipris, J. (2005). *To be a Playwright*. New York: Routledge.

Spencer, S. (2002). *The Playwright's Guidebook*. London: Faber and Faber.

Stephens, S. (2016). *Simon Stephens: A Working Diary*. London and New York: Bloomsbury Methuen Drama.

Svich, C. (2009). 'The Legacy of Maria Irene Fornes: A Collection of Impressions and Exercises'. *PAJ: a Journal of Performance and Art*, 31(3), 1–32.

Sweet, J. (1993). *The Dramatists Toolkit: The Craft of the Working Playwright*. Portsmouth, NH: Heinemann.

Tidmarsh, A. (2014). *Genre: A Guide to Writing for the Stage and Screen*. London: Bloomsbury.

Wandor, M. (2008). *The Art of Writing Drama*. London: Bloomsbury Academic.

Wright, M. (1997). *Playwriting in Process*. Portsmouth, NH: Heinemann.

8

Generating action

*No matter how formally experimental I might have
been with [my plays] ... nevertheless and even in those
plays, they can be described as characters in action
in a situation.*

SIMON STEPHENS

Introduction

The focus for this chapter is action – the energy of characters.
It is the action of the play that engages the audience in the idea.

There are two ways to think about action. The first is the
action within the play – the way characters work to achieve
their goals. The word 'drama' comes from the Greek 'to do'
and the first way to think about action is what the character
is willing to do to achieve their goals – how they attempt
to influence their environment and other characters (or
themselves) in the *fictional* time and space. This is characters
acting on each other.

The second way to think about action is to explore how a
play 'acts' on audience engagement to take them on a theatrical
journey. This meaning explores *dramatic action*, how the
playwright manipulates the elements of drama to create a
theatrical experience for an audience in *actual* time and space.

Part 1: Character action

Action as dialogue and dialogue as action

All action comes from a character trying to get what they want. Everything they do or say must be an action to achieve that want.

As explored in the previous chapter, a play is about characters who want things, encounter obstacles and either succeed or fail in their quest.

Sometimes they say things to get what they want, sometimes they do things.

In this way, dialogue and activity are actions only when they are attempting to achieve specific goals.

Actions reveal, develop and create character. What a character wants and how much they want it (i.e. how high the stakes are) determines *what* they are willing to do and the *kind of language* they will use to achieve it.

Dialogue is a speech act (Wandor, 2008). The reason someone speaks is to influence others to get what they want: the question 'Would you like a cup of coffee?' makes sense when we know the action – is it a request for love, a demand for attention or is the action to caution, insult or flatter? Or does the other character look thirsty? So, the action is to be helpful, to assist.

Plays are about struggle – high stakes struggle – and are made up of action and reaction. And as a character exists in relationship to others, their actions (i.e. dialogue and behaviour) and their responses to the actions of other characters create the engagement for an audience.

Plays are about people: arguing, falling out, wrangling, plotting, deceiving, denouncing, avenging. Sweet (1993, p. 3) suggests that interactions within a play are negotiations over wants and that all conflict begins as a negotiation. These negotiations may appear superficial but should be incredibly important – the text and subtext. Think how divorcing couples fight over possessions – and children – not wanting to 'lose' by giving away their least favourite coffee mug.

As a writer, you need to be clear what your characters want *from each other* at each moment. That is, if you know the want then *what* they say will always be *dramatic* and/or theatrical.

As everything characters do is motivated by some desire or objective, the other character's *response* needs to be motivated as well. Their action is to get what they want or prevent the other character getting what they want.

So, for every line, it helps to see each statement or behaviour as a *tactic* – an attempt to achieve something: sympathy, agreement, guilt, a cup of coffee. If you see every word as a *tactic* your scene will be dramatic and dynamic. Ask: 'What tactic are they employing to get what they want?' This ensures information remains motivated. They are not telling the audience, they are trying to act on another character.

This keeps the 'action' in their interactions. It stops the scene from being about conveying information, discussion or exposition (where the dialogue is really serving the playwright's want for the audience to know something). Lines that tell the audience information, and are not asking/impelling another character to do something, need an edit.

As drama is about struggle and interactions in a world of relationships, after the first line, everything else is a reaction to past or imagined actions[1].

Writing exercise: Verbing the line

As every line is an action, it can be described by a verb.

The use of verbs to ensure action is very effective; if you can't verb the line, that is, determine what the action is behind the words and what the line is doing to the other character(s),

---

[1]Which is another reason why pre-planning, mapping out the whole play and plotting the actions can ensure motivated, not expository, dialogue – showing not telling.

then perhaps the line isn't adding to the action and needs to be modified or cut. Ask:

- What does my character want at this particular moment in time? What is the line/section hoping to achieve?
- What is the desired outcome?
- What *tactic* are they employing to get what they want?
- What 'verb' can you attach to each line of dialogue to explain why they continue to talk or why they remain in the scene?

This also helps with structure: when they achieve their goal they leave – the scene is ended. Similarly, if they realize they can't get what they want they will also leave and end the scene. So, if you get the action right, structure (sort of) looks after itself.

As playwriting is about the present tense (Gooch, 2001), choose 'present tense' verbs.

For example, tactics (or verbs) could be:

to impress	to mother	to question
to invade	to protect	to challenge
to mock	to put down	to reject

For one of your scenes, or an excerpt from a play you know well, write a verb at the end of each line that reveals the action. And if you notice that the verb is the same for two consecutive lines ask yourself 'Is this a choice or am I being lazy? Can I cut the line? Should I change the line to create a more intense level of the same tactic or to create a new tactic all together?' (Of course, repeated tactics are not a problem if they are actively chosen.)

Actions and writing for actors

Even though it is a text that can stand on its own, a play is written to be read and produced by theatre artists. It is to be *acted* and actors need something to do. Actors want more than talking and making tea.

But what that means for the writer changes with the style.

In realist theatre, characters need a reason to act – an 'objective'. An actor needs to know what their character wants – the cliché of the 'what's my motivation' question reflects that a character needs a purpose for being in the scene. Action for a character is linked to their super-objective – what they want by the end of the play/life. Then actors need to know what their character wants at the end of the scene – *a major objective*. And then they need to know what they need at the end of each line – the *immediate objective* (see Chapter 7 for more detail). So, a playwright needs to write with this in mind – not with definitive answers but with plenty of scope for idea generation from directors and actors.

In less realistic and post-dramatic work that may not focus on character or plot, the objective of the action is often directed at the audience. The dialogue or activity may resemble normal speech and behaviour (or not). The figures will 'act' to shock, to challenge, to appease, to amaze, to enlighten the audience and/or other roles/figures/characters. It may be more ritualistic or visceral, but dialogue and activity still create theatrical and/or dramatic action. They create an experience for an audience. In this sense, it may only be possible to talk about the 'action of the performance' and the way each moment creates an audience experience.

Part 2: Dramatic action

This brings us to the other way to think about action, that is, the way playwrights manipulate dramatic and theatrical conventions to generate and maintain audience engagement. In other words, how the play acts on the audience to achieve the playwright's objective. This is the craft that keeps the audience and spectator listening and watching.

The play occurs in real time and space – it has a beginning, a journey for the audience and then an end. The playwright's job is to make choices about the dramatic action to provide the audience with the experience they have imagined.

Like the structure of a scene, and the larger structure of a play, the dramatic action needs to be managed and manipulated to create the desired effect.

If structure describes the release of information or story, that is, the plot, then the dramatic action controls the emotional, visceral and intellectual journey of the audience through a theatrical experience in their seat.

Ultimately, a play's effectiveness, its ability to realize its objectives (the premise or controlling idea), depends on a playwright's ability to control and manipulate theatrical and dramatic tools.

The play's dramatic action and the ways the play manipulates the audience's experience are part of the 'objectives' of the piece.

A play may have multiple 'objectives' – these may be emotional (what the playwright wants the audience to feel?), intellectual (think) and theatrical (experience) or all three complementing each other or with one supporting the other(s).

The kind of dramatic action the playwright creates is determined by the big questions we asked in Chapter 6: What kind of play do I want to write? What kind of experience do I intend for the audience?

A playwright needs to be aware of the relationship between the dramatic action within the fictional world and the theatrical experience for the audience.

A playwright manages an audience's experience through the manipulation of the elements of drama to create the journey through time (the length of the play) that creates an active experience for the audience.

In most plays, a playwright increases audience engagement by placing characters or figures in situations that make achieving their goals increasingly difficult and by placing increasingly difficult obstacles in their path. This action creates tension. Obstacles or complications force characters to react, which causes further conflict. This increasing intensity of action creates suspense.

A play needs to be structured dynamically. The scenes or episodes need to be rhythmically placed alongside each other (Wesker, 2010). The actions in a play are like the components of an equation or a chemical reaction: one leads to another, causing still more. Or we can think of each moment as a domino that knocks the next one over.

In shaping action, playwrights keep the premise or objective of their play in mind, so they are clear what they want to happen in each scene and from their play overall. Key questions to explore dramatic action include the following:

- What do you want to achieve with this scene? For the characters? For the audience?
- What is the key experience or idea you want to explore? How do these scenes create this experience/communicate that idea?
- How do these scenes add to our understanding of what it means to be human?
- What experience do I want the audience to have now, at this moment? And now ... and now?
- This links to considerations of structure – How do you deliver and/or withhold information? What comes first? How do the pieces fit?

Elements of drama

As well as ensuring the scene is theatrical, activities that explore the elements of drama can be used to create new scenes and help students write through a scene they are finding challenging or difficult. For example, using one of the elements to give a scene a self-imposed parameter can help the writer transform an otherwise 'talky' scene into something more dramatic and theatrical.

These exercises can be used in the way musicians use scales to develop skills and craft 'strength'. Encourage students to write early and write often by reminding them that the scenes are unrelated to their current project, and are just skills practice (though if they do write something relevant they can keep it).

Writing exercise: Action and the elements of drama

Set yourself a time limit – say fifteen minutes.

Complete one of the activities from the list below.

Then, after a day or two, try another, but this time give yourself twenty minutes and see if you can finish the scene, that is, bring it to a resolution.

You will be surprised how easy it is to 'practise' writing if you give yourself short assignments.

Write a scene:

- Where the focus is on a non-speaking character. Create a situation where there are several people in the room but one of them doesn't ever speak. Give them the focus.

- Where there is a shift in status and power; for example, where a student gets the better of a principal or a bully is challenged by their victim(s).

- Where time is an obstacle that increases tension or stakes, like a theatrical 'bomb' with a burning fuse: for example, strangers waiting for a train, who strike up a conversation and know it will end when the train arrives; or two 'culprits' trying to get their story straight outside the principal's office knowing they could be called in at any moment.

- Where tension is created when the dialogue ignores an obvious 'elephant in the room': for example, a scene where an unopened (or opened) letter sits on the table that neither character mentions, but they (and we) know, holds a secret; or perhaps only one knows; or maybe one character 'threatens' to open it to tease the other, etc. The letter could be a love note or a speeding ticket, a doctor's bill or something else that one character is ashamed of or unwilling to share with the other.

- Where the mood of the scene contrasts with the text or situation: a sombre birthday party or a frivolous funeral. Keep it subtle and ensure the audience is interested in 'why'.

- That explores stark contrast in characterization. Place two different people in a confined space, or a group of people (nuns or vegetarians) who encounter 'difference' (punks or butchers) in their environment or who travel to another environment (casino or boardroom). What do your characters do? What does it say about them? Other examples could include business executives on a building site, children in a board room, and a teenager and an older person at a bus stop.

- Where the characters fight over an object that is symbolic to one or both, but they won't admit or acknowledge its importance. Encourage high stakes: for example, a scene where a divorcing couple both want the 'ugly' coffee table; or two friends who fight over a piece of clothing (old shirt/sports jersey/jacket) that one lent to the other, but now wants back because they are not friends anymore.

Generating action through environments and place

Most environments have an intended purpose – some 'activity' that is the reason for their existence: laundromat, hairdressers, courtroom, etc. Thus, some situations have inherent actions (as opposed to activity) that supplement, complement or contradict the specific actions of the characters. People go there to perform that action. For example, you go to court to find justice, to prove your innocence, and to do that, you speak and argue, etc. A laundromat has business, folding, etc., but the action is 'to clean' or it may be to escape.

Further, these places or situations have 'climates'– factors that affect business such as open or closed, public and private, noisy or quiet, friendly or hostile, hot or cold.

Therefore place can create business or activity as well as actions, and a playwright can use them to generate complications, struggles and negotiations and to create text as scaffolding for the subtext.

Writing exercise: Action and environment

Use the following as scene starters:

1   An empty laundromat with big glass windows that overlook a busy street.

   It is early evening. Two strangers, A and B.

   One (A) has run out of money but still has a washing machine full of wet clothes.

   The other (B), apparently quiet and reserved, is the only other customer.

   A's 'action' is to avoid embarrassment and to clean clothes. B wants to clean clothes and avoid people.

   Write the scene using all the business and actions implied by the place and situation.

2   A fast-food restaurant with chairs and table. Empty except for Character A, who is eating, Character B, who is waiting to order food, and Character C, who is cleaning the bench. This can go on for as long as you think the audience will accept.

   Character C finally takes the order. Character B realizes they do not have enough money for their order. Character A overhears.

The background is that Character A is in love with Character B.

Character A wants to save face and eat. Character B wants to impress, but not humiliate A. Character C is probably not very helpful – their action is to obstruct. Write the scene using all the stage business a fast-food restaurant provides.

Action, engagement and narrative drive

Even if a playwright has created sufficiently high stakes and engaging characters, unless the audience cares about the action, the play won't maintain their interest. The audience needs to be invested in who wins, who survives, and who maintains integrity, etc.

The play needs to keep the audience 'sitting forward in their seat', actively making sense of the images, words and moments to create meaning from the events on stage.

This can be achieved by narrative. The audience will be engaged by increasing stakes, the tension of wondering what has happened to get to this point, what is *really* happening at this moment, what will happen next to the characters and/or what will happen next, theatrically.

In a realistic play, suspense is created by asking the audience to follow the story and wonder what the narrative turns will be. In Miller's *All My Sons*, the suspense is created by piecing together the back story of illegal and deadly business decisions, and then wondering what this information means for the characters in the play's 'now'.

Writing exercise: Chain of actions

Writing a *chain of actions* can generate character, events and structure.

Begin with a short description of an activity or event from your characters and/or situation, either from a play you are writing or from a scene you have worked on as part of the exercises in this book. For example:

John (father) cleans up after Allan's (son's) party.

Now begin the next sentence with 'So that', exploring John's motive.

Remember to keep the stakes high.

The action might be to save him from embarrassment, or to act the martyr, or to retrieve his bond.

The next sentence introduces a complication. Begin this sentence with 'But then…' and nominate a character (in this case it might be Allan, or it might be one of Allan's friends) to perform an action. For example, Allan arrives home but challenges John.

Then add an event: 'And then'. John ignores Allan.

Continue for as long as you can – pages if possible.

The resulting list contains all the actions the characters do – a skeleton of dramatic structure; you now add the specific dialogue and business that seeks to achieve that 'verb' – a challenge can be active or passive: a silent continuation of some minor business or a violent outburst. The idea is to focus on exploring how complications arise from a character's actions and other character's response to them – a chain of complications and possibilities (which are really complications in disguise).

Moments, not narrative: Action in post-dramatic theatre

In more episodic or non-linear pieces the audience will wonder what the next 'experience' will be – how we, as an audience, will *feel* next and how this string of experiences, that generally occur in linear audience time, adds up to a meaningful yet visceral experience.

The action escalates or, in an episodic play, vacillates but becomes more urgent as the journey of the play continues. In

Mother Courage, we see Mother Courage lose more and more of what is important to her – her children. Even in moments where her possessions seem more valuable to her than a child, we understand that eventually she will be left with nothing but her cart. The journey for the audience is managed, not by narrative suspense but by witnessing the ceaseless attack on an individual by the machine of war and business. Brecht's plays are about characters for whom there appears to be no correct decision, no way to avoid tragedy.

We are also engaged by the epic theatre conventions – devices that manipulate the audience experience to make the theatre experience strange, encouraging rational thought. The conventions are part of the conscious audience experience. We see characters change costume on stage, and we see the lights and other devices that remind us we are at the theatre.

Kaufman (2001) talks about creating 'moments' for the audience that add up to the play's meaning. In a sense, all plays are a series of moments and experiences that lead to an overall 'meaning' for the audience. That meaning may be created through a play of ideas, that makes an audience think, or through creating a character, that makes an audience feel, but they are all a journey of change for the audience. The experience – created viscerally, emotionally or/and intellectually – is a culmination of experiential moments organized in scenes.

The practice of post-dramatic work – with a theatrical piece that is often not mediated by narratives of realistic characters – demonstrates that, ultimately, it is the experience that is the purpose of a night at the theatre – to increase the possibility of empathy, to generate change or create beauty. And for the experience to be lasting, it will need to be visceral – the audience needs to be affected 'in their guts' – otherwise they could have read an article or attended a lecture.

Dramatic writing can learn from the trends or examples of theatre that challenges the assumptions of traditional dramatic thinking. Post-dramatic theatre explores the experiential – that theatre 'works' even if it is primarily or even solely a visceral response – and thus manipulates emotional moments, primal images, the body and non-text art forms (such as dance and performance art) to create their temporal work. This reminds the dramatic writer of the power of image and emotional visceral 'moments' to enrich the theatricality of their play, and as tools to increase the effectiveness of the drama of a written text. It reintroduces the imagination into the mix of tools in our spectrum.

Writing exercise: Moments

Use blank index cards to plot the moments of your play.

What happens to the audience during your play?

This is not plot, but audience experience. What are the high points? Moments of building suspense? Like Freytag's triangle (but not limited by it), try to see the play as a whole.

See if you can plot the action and see how much *actually* happens in each scene. If nothing happens for the audience you might need to add more precise actions.

It may be subtle – or even delayed – but consider how each word or movement is part of a negotiation or a response to conflict.

For example:

   Card 1: Character A enters, sneaking in holding
      their shoes (action = to deceive, audience
      experience = suspense).

   Card 2: This *causes* Character B to wake up, cranky,
      who then yells at Character A (= to reprimand,
      audience = tension).

   Card 3: This makes Character A defensive (= to distract
      or to hide, audience escalating tension) who then
      threatens to leave Character B, etc. (to attack, audience:
      climax).

Improvisation and writing

As discussed in Chapter 9, 'Crafting dialogue', improvisation and workshop writing increase students' awareness of, and skills in, manipulating the elements of drama. To create art, students need to not only understand the art form and its 'tropes', they also need to be taught how to manipulate and control them.

Using the drama workshop as the place to imagine and begin writing helps the student focus on writing for actors in time and space. The improvised scene develops students' skills in creating effective dramatic action, and teaching them the importance of mood, role, tension space, etc. These skills are transferrable to the written scene. When teaching acting in our classes, we teach students to manipulate dramatic action. When we ask them to improvise within a situation, to become characters in relationships, with defined status, who fight for something, we are focusing on action. As we will see below, improvisation for scene work can help a writer keep their work vital and full of action.

And improvising on the workshop floor specifically for the written page explores the embodied endpoint of play texts. This of course needs to be considered in the context of writing for performance – leaving room for directors and actors – but the idea that the written text should generate and manipulate dramatic action, create tension and mood, manipulate time and space, as well as generate symbol and subtext, will focus students on writing theatre, the temporal and experiential as well as intellectual.

Workshop writing can be used at the beginning of the process to generate ideas and develop fundamental skills. Or it can be used in the middle to clarify and refine the scenes and their forward movement. At the end of the process it can be used to see the work as a whole – how the scenes work together. The workshop environment allows writers to observe the scenes they are writing and to see their work as play – improvising and seeing what works (see Chapter 12). While the following exercises are written to be used in a workshop situation, they can, with minor modifications, also be part of your students' individual writing improvisation – completed in their writing journal at home.

Writing exercise: Improvised action

1 *There is something I want you to do but I won't tell you what it is.*

   Think of a situation – a place and two characters, A and B, in a relationship. One student/Character B is sent out of the room (momentarily).

   The other, Character A, is given an unspoken objective that they must play in the scene. They want Character B to do something – apologize, give them a back rub, offer to help them move, call a taxi, order a pizza, etc. The character cannot ask them directly. They must use other ways to get what they want.

   Character B returns. They improvise a scene until Character B has worked out what they are expected to do and, staying in the scene, completes the action, giving the Character A what they want – or not.

   These scenes can begin quite simply, like the suggestions above, but can develop into complex and subtle interactions and manipulations. For example, Character A wants Character B to admit their infidelity or Character A wants Character B to break up with them – knowing that Character B is still very much in love.

2 *Stage business only.*

   Perform a scene in activity/'stage directions' only. Embed the actions in the business/activity.

3 *Action in the business.*

   Improvise a scene where the character can only pursue their action through business/activity. The dialogue

will be a smoke screen – about superficial day to day
things – but the student's body language and activity
will be requesting another.

Summary

- Action can refer to the characters trying to achieve their
  wants. Action is both dialogue and activity.
- Dramatic action refers to the playwright's use of the
  elements of drama to create an audience experience.
- Audiences are engaged through narrative as well
  as through juxtaposition of emotional or theatrical
  moments.
- All plays are experiential and create visceral reactions
- Action can be used to generate ideas for character and
  theme.
- Improvisation, written and acted, can be used to
  generate action to write scenes that are dramatic and/or
  theatrical and engaging.

References

Gooch, S. (2001). *Writing a Play*. London: A & C Black.
Kaufman, M. (2001). *The Laramie Project*. New York: Vintage
  Books.
Sweet, J. (1993). *The Dramatists Toolkit: The Craft of the Working
  Playwright*. Portsmouth, NH: Heinemann.
Wandor, M. (2008). *The Art of Writing Drama*. London:
  Bloomsbury Academic.
Wesker, A. (2010). *Wesker on Theatre*. London: Oberon Books.

9

Crafting dialogue

*It can serve as a way in, writing a great piece of dialogue
between two people but it can't end there … let's get in
and get started and ask what is underneath there what
can we pluck out from there? And remind them that
dialogue may or may not end up in the play – it is not
sacred – just because you wrote it … it's an entry point.*

HILARY BELL

Introduction

The focus for this chapter is dialogue, the sounds and silences
that make up the aural elements of the play.

Dialogue consists of what is said (and what is deliberately
unsaid) by characters to reveal, create and resolve the play's
action.

The sounds, rhythms, intensity and symbolism of the
dialogue contribute to the dramatic action, creating stylized
theatrical moments that go beyond the natural.

As we said in previous chapters:

- A play is about a character who wants something, who
  encounters obstacles and ultimately either succeeds or
  fails in that quest.

- Dramatic action comes from the words and energy that keeps the characters moving and the play engaging.
- All action comes from a character trying to get what they want. Everything they do or say must be an action to achieve that want.

What is dialogue?

Dialogue is the primary component of (most) playwriting – it is how much of the action of your play will be communicated to your audience.

Dialogue is crafted to reveal the following:

- The depth of your characters – their internal life, their dreams and wants, aspirations and limitations.
- Their external identity communicated through how they talk and what words or phrases they choose.
- Their role in the action and the energy that they bring (or remove).

In other words, dialogue has two main functions:

- It develops and reveals character.
- It creates action that furthers the story and the plot/ journey of the play.

If it isn't doing one or both, it needs to be cut.

Dialogue moves the play forward, introducing the key actions that bring objectives into conflict, which in turn generate further conflict. Dialogue is a sequence of speech acts – each line requires and instigates the next. Therefore, all dialogue needs to be focused to further the action of the play and its characters.

Dialogue conveys text and subtext. It may be poetic, stylized or 'realistic', but it is *crafted* to create an impact on the audience. That is, however realistic it may appear, all dialogue is heightened: no dialogue is actually 'real'. It is constructed by playwrights to create a desired impact on an audience. It is all designed to create a *theatrical* experience.

Even verbatim texts are made surreal or unreal by removing the words from their context and time, and representing them in a theatre or performance space. It is an artifice to bring the audience into the action and the lives of the characters.

What can dialogue do?

Dialogue can

- *provide information.*
  Have you seen my keys?

- *encapsulate the relationship between the characters.*
  You always ask me to find your stuff, can't you look after yourself?

- *provide symbolic and sub-textual elements.*
  Well, if you didn't move my stuff all the time, they would be where I left them.

- *create sound and rhythm to maintain interest.*
  (picking them up from the key bowl) These keys, these keys, keys, these ones? Are these the keys you are looking for?

- *reveal character.*
  (beat) You could have just said they were in the bowl at the beginning? You/

- *and further the plot.*
  You've got them now. You can go. Have fun. I will put the kids to bed and clean up. Don't wake me when you come in.

Focus on listening

One way to begin developing students' skills in writing dialogue is to train their ear. Many beginning writers create characters that sound the same – either like the writer or like the group to which the writer belongs/identifies.

Perhaps their words sound like what the writer 'thinks' good dialogue should sound like.

To develop the skills of writing differentiated yet *real* dialogue, students can train their ear – train it to notice the complexities and subtleties of the spoken word and to learn how to manipulate them to create dialogue that generates action, furthers the plot and develops characters.

A way to develop your ability to write dialogue is to listen to people's conversations. Jean Claude van Itallie (1997) explores the benefits of transcribing snippets of 'overheard conversations' to understand the distinct rhythms and peculiarities of the real speech.

Writing exercise: Training the ear[1]

While at home or out (on a train, at a café, bus stop, etc.) listen to a conversation between two or three people. Pay close attention noticing hesitations, grunts, pauses, etc.

When you get home, try and transcribe the conversation as closely as possible.

Look for the following:

1 Unfinished sentences

2 Repetition

3 Responses that show the people are not really listening to each other

4 Non-verbal speech acts

---

[1]Adapted from van Itallie, *The Playwright's Handbook* (1997).

5 Different 'voice' of each person – choice of words, length of sentences, etc.

6 Errors and mispronounced words.

Reading it back, what do you notice? How exciting would that be as a play text? What would you need to do to make it more engaging dramatic and theatrical?

Real speech and theatre speech

As the last exercise showed you, real speech is peppered with errors, repetition, unfinished sentences and interruptions. People in life don't always make sense, they talk over each other and often don't finish their thoughts. There can even be a sense of aimlessness about real conversation.

Dialogue is carefully written and rewritten to remove the 'boring' bits – that is, the dialogue that doesn't have an objective – and to cut out *most* of the fillers – the 'umms' and 'ahhs', repetitions and false starts that are not needed to further the action or reveal character or subtext.

The paradox is that for crafted dialogue to ring *true* it needs to *sound* slightly 'flawed'. Realistic dialogue must appear to be the spontaneous words of a character responding to the ideas and actions/interactions in the scene. As Sweet (1993) suggests, the playwright needs to create the illusion of spontaneity. For example, some of the wanderings and lack of clarity in real speech can be used in a scene to further the action or our understanding of the characters, to increase conflict as well as to give the conversations the appearance of people finding words within the reality of the conversation. Further, audiences read characters who reveal their emotions too easily as being insincere, which may or may not be what the writer wants.

Life amplified

Theatrical life is 'amplified'. It is based on *real* interactions but, as Stoppard (Guppy, 1988) said, dialogue needs *an imposed* sense of drama.

A scene and its dialogue are more concentrated than life. They are intense and complex and the dialogue can perform several functions at once – what Rivera (in Herrington and Brian, 2006) considers maximum density.

A playwright can concentrate time and increase the level of conflict in a scene much more quickly than you would expect from real life. They can escalate interactions more quickly, leaving out steps and trusting that the audience will keep up. In some ways, underwriting dialogue allows the audience a more active role: they will lean in a bit, as having to piece together what is happening keeps them engaged.

Writing exercise: Theatricalize the everyday

Rewrite the conversation you transcribed in overheard conversation, removing random mistakes and repetitions, etc. Then consciously reintroduce some of the tropes of real speech to create action: 'umming' and 'ahhing' to avoid a difficult question, repetition as passive aggression – or overt aggression.

The reality of the scene is no longer important – theatricalize the everyday. You need not stay true to the actual intent of the original participants – this is now a writing exercise.

Dialogue creates character

The 'how' of a character's dialogue – word choice, accent, etc. – reveals information about a character that complements and parallels the meaning of their words – the 'what'.

The rhythm, patterns and sound of a character's speech communicates meaning about their role in the play and their intentions and actions.

As Sweet (1993) explains, one way to explore how dialogue reveals character is to explore which aspects are 'permanent' and which are temporary.

Permanent: Background and context

Clearly, the way a person speaks is affected by who they are and where they come from.

Dialects, local accents and jargon are ways to communicate the context of the character and their world.

Depending on the duration of the play's timeline, a character's accent or background, age and class are generally permanent for the course of the play.

Accents affect syntax. To avoid phonetic approximations, write an accent through word choice and rhythms – trust that an actor will create the sounds. Similarly, other aspects – age and culture – can be embedded in the syntax and diction of the dialogue.

If you chose to write about people from a specific group, then research is necessary to ensure they sound as they should. Yet, as is often the case, theatrical 'truth' might be a little less (or a little more) extreme than reality. If a play replicated the exact speech patterns and phrases of a backyard BBQ from certain parts of Australia an audience would not believe – or even understand – it!

However, character dialogue can be written to reflect exact reality. As has been the constant theme of this book, these suggestions explore the range of choices available to the writer across a spectrum of styles and techniques – principles rather than rules. A writer needs to be aware of what they are saying and be deliberate in their choices. For instance, many people in the same place actually do sound the same, reflecting their membership of a group or community, or a moment in time. In some instances, it makes sense to write short staccato lines for teenage boys, who never want to appear too keen or who actually are not that keen. To make them sound the same shows their allegiance to each other; so when you alter this assumption, you make a statement. As audiences expect everything to mean something, when characters sound the same, it needs to be intentional and significant – and if it isn't, it will be read as a shortcoming.

Despite my statements about teenage boys, the skill is to avoid stereotyping and diminishing a group by oversimplifying – even in a tight group not everyone speaks exactly the same. This is where it is important to research the way people speak to ensure you are as authentic as needed by the script.

Writing exercise: Dialogue accent and dialect

Search YouTube for interviews or news programmes from the area or era you are writing about and immerse yourself in the sounds and rhythms of that 'real' speech.

Listen at length. Then transcribe some (or a great deal) of the speech to see what it looks like on the page. Get an idea of key words and how the sentences are structured. Become clear that you need to create the feel and tone of that speech – not the exact reality. How might this inform the way your characters interact?

Use the ideas from the transcriptions to write a monologue from one of your characters or from someone who represents one of the particular groups you are writing about.

Temporary: Emotional state

A character's emotional state is temporary. And how they are feeling at that precise moment, and why, will affect the way they speak.

How calm they are will influence the way they react to other characters and how they deliver their words. Situations of high anxiety can restrict free-flowing speech or create verbal diarrhoea, so knowing how they are feeling will help you know how to write appropriate dialogue for your characters.

Your character may be out of their normal 'context' which will affect the way they speak, like when a young person meets a mayor, or the mayor goes to a school (see 'Status' in

Chapter 7). So, if a situation creates stress, it can be reflected in dialogue (and clearly, the level of stress can be communicated to the audience by the way a character speaks).

A character's emotional state changes from scene to scene, context to context. As characters interact, their state of mind (as revealed in their pace, rhythm, repetition, syntax, etc.) will impact the other characters, further influencing their responses to words and actions – whether they understand the reason for the stress or not. And trying to understand might be the game of the scene.

Therefore, to understand the impact of emotional states on dialogue and action, think about what your characters are about to do in your scene. Are they nervous because of what they are about to say? How does that affect the way they speak?

Writing exercise: Stressful monologue

Write a monologue (from scratch or for a character in a play you are writing) that begins immediately after:

1 Witnessing a car (empty) being crushed by an elephant that had escaped from a circus.
2 Handing in their resignation letter to a boss they hate.
3 Being sacked from a job they love ... or they hate.
4 Being dumped by someone they really love.
5 Winning the lottery when they are about to be evicted from their home.

Imagine the impact this would have on their emotional state and write a monologue where they recount what has just happened.

These monologues should strengthen your understanding of emotional stress on pace and diction, etc. They will not end up in your play unless they spark a great new idea and/or direction.

Character voices and the playwright's *voice*

In a first draft, characters can often sound the same.

Unless you are making a definite stylistic or thematic choice, realistic characters need character-specific dialogue. Even within an identifiable group or tribe, every character, consciously or unconsciously, has a unique syntax and a vocabulary. Every person speaks in a unique way – often repeating words they like or choosing sentence structures that reflect their personality. Some people talk too much, giving away more than they should; others use words as weapons.

You need to be able to know who is talking by what they are saying and how they are saying it. The character's words reflect who they are – their personal as well as social/cultural background. A parent will only sound the same as their teenage child if they are trying too hard – which could be an interesting choice – or if they are trying to manipulate their child. Again, all these choices are available to the writer as long as they are aimed at achieving a want for the character, and the writer is conscious of the effect they will have on the audience.

Writing exercises: Character voice

1   Write a scene where one character has a distinct verbal quirk or signature style of speech. They might have a favourite word or phrase they return to or they may always end their sentences with a question. See how far you can push it and still sound like real speech.

2   Find a play *you love* – choose any page and, while covering the character names on the left, see if you can identify who is talking by how they speak. Write out all the lines from one character on one page then another character from the same section on another. Compare: what do you notice?

3   Write ten- to- fifteen-line monologues for each of the
    following: a character who

   a   uses street slang well (you might need to research
       this);

   b   uses it badly;

   c   repeats phrases, unconsciously or consciously, such
       as 'You know what I mean?';

   d   sounds like they struggle with the order of their
       words because they are

       i   pre-occupied
       ii   trying to be more impressive;

   e   never finishes a thought.

Exposition and levels of familiarity

Understanding the impact of context on dialogue writing can
help the young playwright determine when and how to manage
exposition in the play – knowing how to include information
that is needed by the audience, but in a way that is part of the
action of a scene.

In any play there are characters who know each other well
and others who may be strangers. Realistically, most of your
characters will be closer than strangers but less than completely
intimate. The level of familiarity determines how characters
speak to each other.

Imagine there being three levels: (1) high familiarity – where
characters know the most about each other; (2) somewhere in
the middle – some detail but also some secrets; and (3) low
familiarity – acquaintances or even strangers.

A playwright can use this concept to determine how much
information is reasonable for one character to share with
another and thus with an audience. The amount of information
needed *by the characters* determines what will be acceptable to
an audience.

In other words, if there is information needed by the audience then make sure there is a newcomer to the group who needs to be introduced to the family or the business or the tragedy that befell the town/school/community before they arrived. Used sparingly, this device will mean that information will be accepted by the audience as it is motivated by the needs of the play rather than *obvious* exposition.

Similarly, if focused on their objectives, characters will naturally include the necessary information to argue their point. Highly intimate situations will include specifics if they are used as weapons or defence; for example, 'that time you got drunk and drove home without me' is a barbed attack – but also reveals character traits and history.

Similarly, lovers with high familiarity would not say something like 'as I was born in Washington, then I …'. Writing will sound forced if the wrong level of intimacy is attributed to the characters and the dialogue. As Sweet (1993, p. 69) warns, the writer's low-context relationship with the audience shouldn't trick them into writing low-context dialogue for characters who have a high-context relationship. Married people know where and when their marriage took place (though if you write that one character forgets where they were married you are making a strong statement to the audience). School friends will know who their teacher is and where their school is located, but might not know who is going out with whom. Workmates don't need to be reminded of the day's routines, but may not know that a co-worker is widowed or dyslexic or vegetarian. Complete strangers and travellers need as much information as the audience, but will be unwilling to share intimacies unless there is a specific reason, such as being lost on an island, trapped in a lift, in an interview situation or if they are starved of intimacy in their other life.

If all else fails, as Catron (2002) suggests, if you have to include some detail or information, hide it in the middle of the line!

Writing exercise: Familiarity

Imagine the situation where one character tells another character

a they are leaving school;
b they are very sick;
c they have won the lottery.

Write the interaction from three levels of familiarity:

a to their parent/best friend/partner;
b to a work colleague;
c to a stranger at the bus stop/waiting room.

How does the character reveal the information? Why do they tell these people? What does it take to tell the stranger? Work mate? How does it change the dialogue (words, rhythm etc.)?

Dialogue is always an interaction

As these levels of familiarity suggest, characters develop and change depending on the context – and who they are speaking to – linking to our understanding of character as a mask. And, as dialogue is a character's attempt to achieve their objectives, what a character says about and to another character communicates the complexities and subtleties of that relationship.

As Wandor (2008) argues, the interaction of two psychologically developed characters often leads to interactions that may seem unusual for either characters in isolation but are believable in context. When realistic characters talk to each other they create interactions that writers may not have predicted.

The theatrical reality of characters interacting to pursue their objectives is that they often don't say what they mean or what they really want. The internal conflict created by their hierarchy of contradictory wants or their understanding of status and context mean that writers need to manage the levels of contradiction and understand how to control the levels of meaning. Contradictions between what the characters say they want and what the audience knows they want develops rich dramatic irony. Playing with subtext allows students to plant 'aha' moments for audiences when they realize that the characters are saying one thing but are really meaning something else.

Writing exercise: Subtext

This exercise will develop your skill in writing layered dialogue.

You will write a series of 'subtext' lines – that is, the meaning underneath the text. Choose key phrases that someone might want to communicate to someone else but are too afraid or unwilling to say out loud. Then you write the text that they actually say, that hides or softens their real thoughts.

Below is a chart with the skeleton of an interaction between two travellers.

The context is they are looking for their hotel in a foreign country. It is mid-/late evening and they are not sure where they are. They know each other well.

Fill out the 'text' column as the characters try to hide their anxiety from the other by, say, focusing on the map and/ or finding public transport. It is also an opportunity to use business as action. The way the characters deal with the map – or passers-by – reflect the subtext as much as their words.

Characters	Subtext	Text
John	I'm scared	
Mary	You're ok	
John	I am scared	
Mary	You're being silly	
John	That upsets me	
Mary	I am getting annoyed	
John	I'm scared	
Mary	I'm not doing this	
John	Tell me it is ok?	

This exercise, while a little unsubtle, encourages you to be aware that characters often don't say what they really mean.

Dialogue as music

As all dialogue is crafted to impact the audience the content of the words is not the only consideration.

The way words sound together is important in writing dialogue in all forms of theatre. Dialogue has a sound and rhythm that evokes and creates meaning. Words have sounds and percussive quality and when you join them together they have a rhythm.

At the most basic level, some words sound so 'right' together they become clichés, so students should be encouraged to avoid words that just seem to go together. Perhaps changing phrases that 'fit like a glove' will have the audience listening to the words and not being distracted by noticing a cliché.

Writing exercise: The music of dialogue

Read a scene you have written (or have studied) out loud to hear the words and their rhythms.

Either record your voice or have others read your words and focus on listening to the 'music' and identify phrases or words that are, perhaps, beautiful on the page but difficult to say. Or identify themes in sounds that reveal character or create mood in the scene or just sound good together and keep the audience in a moment.

Develop these sounds and themes in your characters' dialogue in your next draft of your play.

New language playwrights – riffing and juxtaposition

In more stylized or non-realistic plays, the sounds of the words and the connotations (as opposed to denotations) and associations have a significant impact. Plays with episodic or non-linear narratives and non-realistic characters can use the sound of the words to create mood and moments that contribute to the action in non-traditional ways.

These new techniques, challenging traditional dramaturgy, can be used in dramatic works. They encourage young writers to explore the music of words to complement their meaning, focusing again on audience and theatricality. The approach in its postmodern energy and willingness to break the rules also encourages students to be creative – to play with strange combinations and challenge expectations. It also reminds students of the ritual and poetic nature of interactions in theatre.

Castagno (2001) explores the benefits of riffing – borrowed from jazz improvisation – where the writer plays with repetitions and the sounds of the words to convey 'moments' that create the desired emotional or metaphoric experience for the audience. Often experimenting with meta-theatricality – drawing attention to the play as a play – these techniques also explore clashes of register or 'time' in language to create a multi-vocal character with the breaking of norms drawing attention to the sound and meaning of their words. Think about how the repetitive interactions in Beckett's *Waiting for Godot* and Stoppard's *Rosencrantz and Guildenstern Are Dead* use this technique to impact the form of the play which in turn underlines the existential questions of the texts. The form – for example, repetition – is part of the meaning.

On a more character-focused level, action and/or conflict can be created by juxtaposing contrasting levels of language to 'show' that characters get on each other's nerves without the content of the dialogue addressing this conflict. For example, conflict between a pompous character and a working-class character can be demonstrated by choosing to have them not meet in the middle – both holding on to the jargon of their position as acts of defiance. A resolution to the conflict can be shown when one of them uses the other's phrases etc.

The conscious clashing of class register or local dialects can prompt the audience to reflect on the reasons behind these differences or the history and future of relationships between groups. The sounds become emblematic of class or structures complementing then enriching the ideas in the play.

Writing exercises: Dialogue riffing

1   Choose a word whose sound you particularly like (my favourite is palaver).

    Say it many times, in as many different ways as you can, until it no longer seems to make sense.

    Improvise a conversation where A and B argue over whose turn it is to take out the garbage and they can only use that word.

2   Find your favourite long word.

    Now break it down into its syllables – its core sounds – and play with that.

    In the Australian play *7 Stages of Grieving* by Wesley Enoch and Deborah Mailman, there is a scene that explores the word *reconciliation*, and turns it into *wreck on silly nation* – playing with the sound to create new meaning(s).

3   Improvise/write a scene that plays with syllables and sentence length.

    Begin an interaction between siblings as they negotiate who gets to/has to buy their parent's Christmas/ anniversary present (they both either want it or both don't want it).

    As the intensity increases, so does the length of the sentences. If they feel they are winning they use soft long words, and if they feel they are losing they use short hard words.

4   Improvise/write a character who mainly uses monosyllabic/sharp words.

Write a monologue where, for example, a sports star brags about their skills yet reveals limited abilities with language.

5 Improvise/write an interaction between two strangers who meet on a plane.

They fight for status by trying to speak with the most complicated words. Every time they hesitate they need to go back to short sharp sentences. As they feel more 'impressed' by what they have said, their sentences can lengthen and incorporate more complex structures and words.

Punctuation as notation

The use of precise punctuation in dialogue, while appearing old fashioned, is important for new writers. Albee argued that theatre is a heard experience (hence audience). The writer uses specific punctuation to manage the rhythm and sound of the words and to communicate to an actor and director clues to timing in a scene. Like a composer to a conductor, the play's punctuation indicates how the piece is to sound and the obvious implications for meaning. As Mamet (1998) suggests, punctuation isn't pedantry but part of the story, part of the information created by the text.

Young writers should consider punctuation as notation for the music of their words. Punctuation tells an actor how to create the rhythm to emphasize the words and ideas that are needed to make the scene clear and effective. A question means something quite different to an unsure statement.

Be careful not to over-punctuate – too many exclamation marks disappear, as they are ignored.

And punctuation is only effective when it is text, not direction. Consider the use of ellipsis and contractions to create opportunities for subtext, tension, poor communication between characters: but use them precisely and sparingly.

Stage directions

Stage directions are often a trap for young writers. There is a temptation to use stage directions as a way to give advice to an actor but there is no need to make acting choices for the performers. *Warmly* or *aggressively* may not be very helpful. Let the clarity of your word choice do that for you.

The more precise you are in the choice of words, their rhythm and sound, and the more deliberate you are with your choice of punctuation to give the sentences their speed and rhythm, the better you are at highlighting the action.

Similarly, directions regarding set are best when they create the mood of the piece for the designers. Specific details are only necessary if they become part of the action. As Chekhov's gun reminds us, if you specify an object in your script (a gun in this case) the audience will expect it to be integral to the action, or to character or theme, etc.

However, stage directions as action can communicate to an audience character, place, motivation – all without a word being spoken. The final moment of Beckett's *Waiting for Godot* demonstrates the richness of the interaction between stage directions and spoken text – the spoken intention to leave followed by a contradictory stage direction encapsulates much of the meaning of the whole play.

Writing exercise: Stage directions

Hilary Bell explains an exercise using stage directions.

The idea is to write the skeleton or scaffold of a play through stage directions – seven or ten or whatever – and one of the stage directions needs to be 'impossible'.

And they will come up with something that either is or isn't impossible, … but they will come up with something pretty striking: 'the sea sets on fire' or 'she turns into a pile of ashes'. And that image may not necessarily end up in the play, but the idea behind it might – and if nothing else, what that idea does is lend a heightened theatrical sense to the whole play.

So, if you have got two people chatting over a glass of wine, but at a certain moment his chair explodes – that is going to infuse the play with something that is bigger than just normal life and it is also going to make you ask 'What does that mean? Is he just too excited? Is he sitting on something hot?'

When to begin writing the dialogue

The answer to the question 'when' to begin writing dialogue is not simple and depends on the temperament and skill of the student.

I am referring not to dialogue generated in writing exercises or as part of the playwright's process of developing character, but the actual play – what we would call a first draft.

However, there is one caveat. As new playwrights, students tend to overwrite. The joy of writing well-structured and ornate conversations or long monologues can get in the way of action. Young playwrights can be quite accomplished writers and find it difficult to discard their beautiful words.

It is not the quality of the writing necessarily that determines whether it stays in the play or not, but it is its value to the chosen vehicle, action or character. Often if they begin without preparation they become attached to their words even if they do not fit the play they want to write. You need to be conscious that they can fall in love with their words despite them not actually being any good for them. They need to be able to see them objectively, to be prepared to kill their darlings.

Students need to be wary of free-flowing stream of consciousness dialogue. Pages of conversation can seem like a play text, but it is not. Stream of consciousness writing is always a first draft and will need what Gooch (2001) calls conscious shaping to structure the inspirational flow. For some, dialogue writing may be easy, but may delay the creation of action.

Embodied writing – improvisation and the drama workshop

Instead of thinking of playwriting as an easy, stream of consciousness writing process that lets the muse speak through the pen, as I suggested last chapter, I encourage students to think of playwriting as improvisation on the page.

The rules of improvisation free the imagination. For instance, we know the parameters of a scene – characters who have a relationship, who are in a situation, who struggle in pursuit of conflicting objectives. On the page, all this can be made clear, quickly, through motivated dialogue just as easily as on the floor in a workshop. While I spend some time on the playwriting workshop in Chapter 12, I recommend teachers use improvised writing workshops to generate rather than just refine ideas, characters and situations.

As Sweet (1993) argues, the principles of effective improvisation can and should be applied to writing. Adapting acting exercises to teach the craft of writing recognizes the theatrical rather than literary nature of the playwriting process.

As drama educators, we structure workshop activities in our lessons to scaffold the creation of drama and theatre – often spontaneous and devised. The Australian playwright Lachlan Philpott suggests that it was his own experiences as a drama teacher that helped him be an effective playwriting teacher: 'Drama teachers are good at adapting exercises to a different purpose, so an acting activity becomes a writing exercise.' As Gooch (2001, p. 60) suggests, when a playwright improvises, they are 'inside' all the characters in the scene/play and when they read back they are outside the action as writer again. But he also reminds us that, like improvised scenes in workshops, much improvisation feels better from within than it does from outside. As always, the writer needs to evaluate the gold and wash away everything else, then add more gold to these ideas and so on.

Writing exercise: Dialogue writing workshops

There is great merit in hearing the work early, not as a 'draft' of a play but as an interaction, a struggle and a clash of objectives. This workshop will help generate ideas and words – it is about creation not evaluation – to look for the gold.

The writing workshop allows you to:

- hear the words and silences, the gaps as much as the content;
- hear as an actor and an audience – not to find faults but to find what works and to make the work more layered and rich;
- listen to the beginnings and the ends of lines;
- look for poetry and banality;
- listen for how the words fit in the mouth of an actor – and whether this brings character or symbol;
- grab the spontaneous additions to the scene – keep it going or keep it going in your own head;
- listen for trigger words, for symbol, situation, text and subtext.

As you see your scene being workshopped, ask the following questions:

1   Have I made my dialogue naturalistic – with some repetitions and unfinished lines?
2   Have I cut out the unnecessary steps to get to the conflict/complications?
3   Are my characters distinct in their rhythms and word choice?
4   Can I introduce key words or phrases to 'show' my characters more effectively?

5 Can I hear the rhythms of the speech?

6 Are my close relatives telling each other information they would already know?

7 Can I tell how educated my characters are by listening to them? Can I tell where they are from?

8 Can I tell how they are feeling? Are they agitated and is that 'shown through the dialogue? Are they angry? Calm? How is this shown in their word choice? Their sentence structure/syntax?

Summary

- Dialogue has two main functions:
  - It develops and reveals character.
  - It creates action that furthers the story and the plot/ journey.
- All dialogue is crafted to generate the action that drives the play.
- Realist dialogue needs to balance the appearance of reality and the needs of the play.
- Playwrights can use dialogue to generate and communicate character – by either 'permanent' features (accents dialect, etc.) or temporary aspects (emotion/mood, etc.).
- Dialogue is always an interaction, and the level of familiarity can be used to convey motivated information – avoiding clumsy exposition.
- Dialogue is also musical, and playing with the rhythms and sounds of words attends to an audience's need to listen to the play and be engaged by the ideas and the experience.
- Stage directions, when used creatively, can add to the theatricality and create action in movement and visual symbol.

References

Castagno, P. (2001). *New Playwriting Strategies: A Language-Based Approach to Playwriting*. New York: Routledge.

Catron, L. E. (2002). *The Elements of Playwriting*. Long Grove, IL: Waveland Press, Inc.

Gooch, S. (2001). *Writing a Play*. London: A & C Black.

Guppy, S. (1988). 'Tom Stoppard, The Art of Theatre No. 7'. *The Paris Review* (109). Retrieved from https://www.theparisreview.org/interviews/2467/tom-stoppard-the-art-of-theater-no-7-tom-stoppard

Herrington, J. and Brian, C. (Eds). (2006). *Playwrights Teach Playwriting: Revealing Essays by Contemporary Playwrights*. Hanover, NH: Smith and Kraus.

Itallie, J.-C. v. (1997). *The Playwright's Workbook*. Montclair, NJ: Applause Theatre and Cinema Books.

Mamet, D. (1998). *Three Uses of the Knife*. New York: Columbia University Press.

Sweet, J. (1993). *The Dramatists Toolkit: The Craft of the Working Playwright*. Portsmouth, NH: Heinemann.

Wandor, M. (2008). *The Art of Writing Drama*. London: Bloomsbury Academic.

10

Building structures

You know you've got to have an eye on where you are going, a bit, but not too much. It's got that balance that's the spark ... it's like you're in a jungle and there's just rope that you are following and you have one hand quite loosely on the rope, but the rope is quite slack ... you have a rope, because otherwise it can be quite scary, but you can sort of wander – because it doesn't feel good when it feels too tight, but then if it is too loose it is formless [rubbish].

POLLY STENHAM

Introduction

In Chapter 8, I talked about how the wants of the character met with complications and obstacles, creating dramatic tension and energy that drives the action of the play.

The structure of the play is the form imposed by the playwright, as Simon Stephens suggests, to organize this energy.

Structure can refer to the individual scenes, or the overall form of the piece, or the way the story is told. These all have to do with how a playwright delivers and/or withholds information, and the way the narrative and ideas are scaffolded.

Linked to dramatic action, structure impacts how the audience experiences the play in real time. To keep these structural decisions theatrical, the playwright will again ask questions that focus on audience experience: What do I want my audience to know now, at this moment and then here and then again here?

This chapter will look at scene structure, play structure and story structure.

Understanding the scene

While understanding structure *can* help the playwriting student, in many ways, the structure of a scene or a play comes from the action. The structure of a scene follows the patterns set up by the characters struggling to achieve their wants. As Spencer (2002, p. 105) suggests, students looking for advice regarding structure is often code for asking 'What should I write?' His advice is to focus on learning scene structure – action, conflict and event. At its core, a scene is a struggle. Internally, dramatically, it is about *negotiations* (Sweet, 1993, p. 13) – about power, information, status.

Scene structure is based on movement. There must be some change or transformation by the end of the scene. A scene ends when the characters have achieved, or realized they won't achieve, their goal – thus the action continues until there is a realization or an achievement.

From a structural point of view, a scene, like a play, needs a beginning, a middle and an end. To help a young playwright understand what that means, I use an analogy of a bowl of apples.

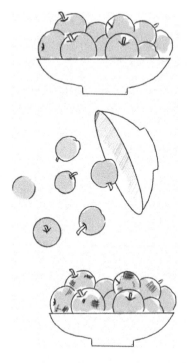

FIGURE 10.1 *The apple bowl.*

The apple bowl	A scene
The apple bowl is over stacked or contains a nearly rotten apple.	A scene begins in a situation of charged balance – the status quo is unstable precarious and perhaps volatile.
Something happens… The whole bowl is toppled, with apples rolling everywhere or you notice the rotten apple and unpack the bowl to remove it.	Something happens… Within that scene an event or action takes place to challenge that balance presenting a complication.

The apple bowl	A scene
You try to put all the apples back in the bowl collecting the runaway from under the table – removing the dirt – a little rub on the shirt – or you identify and remove the rotten apple hopefully before it infects others. You put the apples back in the bowl.	The scene continues as that event is dealt with – actions by characters to return the scene to its original balance – or to guide the scene to the new one.
You chase an apple under the fridge or it's taken by the dog. More apples are identified as rotten.	Further complications will/ may evolve from these actions that require further actions.
All apples are back in the bowl. Some are a little bruised and they are either returned to their precarious stacking or repacked to make it more secure.	Attempts to restore/repair are either successful or not but a new balance is established.

Every moment in a scene is an attempt to restore, repair or accelerate the impact of the complication.

This apple bowl image provides a useful lens for students when redrafting and provides another perspective to ensure a scene is dramatic/theatrical. It gives teachers a vocabulary to discuss the abstract concept of structure, asking:

- What is the opening balance?
- Why is it charged?
- What upsets it?
- What actions does this disruption cause?
- What is the new 'situation'? What new disruptions/ complications does it create?
- When does a scene end? Why now? Why here?

Traditionally, a new scene was thought to begin when someone entered and ended when someone exited. This signifies the beginning of a new struggle or the end of the current one. That is, once a character has no more action, they leave the stage.

Jennifer Tuckett (2017) calls the elements of a scene 'want, conflict and event' with event referring to the change that ends a scene, sending the play in a new direction. This new direction is the reason for the next scene.

Writing exercise: The scene

Begin this lesson with a physical warm-up – a running and image-creating game like statue tag and tableaux.

Then create an exercise that encourages impulse and non-verbal communication – a game. The one I use is called group decision-making. Without discussion and in silence the class is required to form shapes – initially numbers and letters (e.g. make the letter W) then objects (a piano, Formula 1 racing car, a famous bridge – in Sydney, I use the Harbour Bridge and Sydney Opera House).

Then, again as a whole class, students are asked to create an environment – a bank, a diner, a department store. Ask them to remember exactly where they are and who is around them.

This is the charged precarious opening.

Then they walk around the room. Now call for them to imagine an event or a complication that happens in that environment. As a group and without discussion, they depict that event. As they are experienced in following instincts and reading offers they all create a new moment. Unpack what you see – reading the moment they have created, exploring the complication. Remind them to remember where they are and who is near them

After another walk around the room ask them to depict the resolution. What was the response to the complication?

Ask them to repeat the three moments in order – balance, complication and then resolution. Explore how the scene will be written. What are the actions that take the scene from the opening moment through the complication and the attempts to address the event, and then the final resolution?

The play ...

Just like dramatic action, the overall structure of a play creates the audience's journey in time – minute by minute. Structuring the work – how and when information is revealed and how and when characters are introduced – is how a playwright manipulates that experience. How a playwright creates theatrical moments and symbols to complement, juxtapose and parallel the *information* in the text all contribute to the success of the play.

Freytag's (1900) ideas have had a significant impact on the teaching and learning of creative writing. For playwriting purposes, the general structure is helpful, but we need to add more specific information.

The opening of a play needs to communicate a great deal to the audience: the world we will be experiencing, who might we meet in that world, and the rules they will play by (characters and playwright). The opening moments communicate style

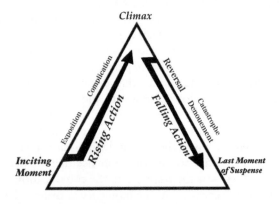

FIGURE 10.2 *Freytag's pyramid as a model for standard story format (adapted from Freytag, 1900, pp. 114–40).*

and genre to orient how the spectators/audience read the play. As Gooch (2001) suggests, the beginning of the play will 'present us with an event or situation which introduces us immediately to the heart of the plays conflict' (p. 79). Sweet agrees, suggesting that the first few pages of a play need to be carefully crafted to ensure 'they correctly establish the world and style of the two hours to follow' (1993, p. 66).

'How to begin?' Or is the question 'when to begin?'

One common principle to ensure dramatic engagement is to 'get in late, leave early' – the audience needs to arrive in the middle of something. Gooch (2001) likens it to jumping on a moving bus. In the apple analogy, we don't need to see the apples being bought or even stacked in the bowl.

In many ways a play needs to mirror the structure of a scene.

Like a scene, a play begins in a precarious balance, before it is challenged by a complication. Many call this the inciting incident (see Catron, 2002).

In a conventional play, this disruption starts the action of the play by setting off a chain of events that throw the world into upheaval.

The inciting incident – the change in the equilibrium – can come from any number of sources. It can be a character's action (King Lear, the Ghost in *Hamlet*), a change in an environment (*The Tempest*), a change in dynamic (Catherine getting a boyfriend in *A View from a Bridge*) or a larger conflict impacting relationships (the family feud in *Romeo and Juliet*). However, as we see in all these examples, the specific incidents are all exacerbated by the greater context – a play is almost always about more than its specifics.

In many great plays, this incident may have occurred quite a long time before the events of the play – Nora's forged signature in *A Doll's House* and the military armament deals in *All My Sons* are good examples.

In others, while recent, the inciting incidents happen before the opening scene – think both the King's murder and the hasty remarriage in *Hamlet* and Othello's marriage to Desdemona.

And for some, the incident is within the opening of the play, such as King Lear's decision to divide the kingdom. Lear's request, that his daughters profess their love for him before he hands out the (predetermined?) allocations of the kingdom, upsets the volatile status quo and reveals the tensions and fractures within the family. It invites the further complication of Cordelia's response and another when Kent intervenes. Lear's response to these disruptions – trying to regain the 'balance' where he has the power – creates greater complications, including banishments and humiliating requests to his daughters, that demonstrate his weakness and allow them to 'insult' him further.

The play follows the same 'apple bowl' analogy and can be examined using the same questions used for a scene.

The key structural question for your play is: Why *now*? Why are we beginning *here*? At this moment? At this time in the world you have created? What is special about this night, this day?

Which is why there is often a precise moment that tips the balance.

For example, Polly Stenham's *That Face* begins with the scene of Mia's misconduct at the elite boarding school. This incites the action of the play because, as the school contacts Mia's mother, it exposes the dysfunction of the domestic situation, and Martha's 'issues'. This event also brings Mia home, to upset the balance in the apartment, and then the events unfold. As the situation worsens, the estranged father returns, and the status quo is irrevocably broken – the apples are all over the floor.[1]

---

[1]Polly Stenham has also carefully included a nice detail to show 'context': it is Mia's overuse of her mother's sedatives that causes the ritualized initiation to go wrong and Martha is present in the incident that brings her down.

How to continue ... selecting the moments to include

As we learn in Chapter 8, the play is a chain of actions and reactions/coactions that present complications or possibilities (which, as I said, are disguised complications anyway).

Structuring those moments can be as simple as a linear progression. The chain of events is like dominoes – one action knocking over the next, creating actions that knock over others and so on. And each moment needs to pass their 'Why this moment?' question. Structurally, a play doesn't include every minute of a story, but needs to choose the days that show the characters at their most stressed, most extreme, most joyous, to motivate some larger action – to focus the experience you want for the audience.

However, while one action must cause the next in the structure *of the story*, the structure of the play can reorder that sequence to change the audience experience of the characters or the issue. As Aronson (2000) suggests, all non-linear plots still have a chronological linear narrative that has just been reordered. *Betrayal* by Harold Pinter structures the narrative in reverse to manage audience access to information and their engagement with characters and ideas.

Further, the events and situations can be placed not in sequence but in juxtaposition. Kaufman (2001) in *The Laramie Project* adopts a less linear structure, creates 'moments' or 'units of theatrical time' that are then juxtaposed with other units to convey meaning' (p. xiv). While they tell their own story, the overall experience is created by how they fit together and how the emotions (rather than the narrative information) of each scene build.

Epic and post-dramatic structures encourage the audience not to ask what happens next but what happens elsewhere (Grace and Bailey, 2016, p. 96). Linked by an idea or a theme, non-traditional works span time and place, asking spectators/ audiences to create meaning by actively making connections between the scenes (Grace and Bailey, 2016).

Either episodic or linear, as our discussion of dramatic action suggests, a play needs to be structured dynamically. The scenes or episodes need to be placed alongside each other conscious of their rhythm (Wesker, 2010).

Writing exercise: The class play

This structure, quite familiar to our students as experienced play builders, can be used in a playwriting classroom to structure the teaching and learning activities to create a performance of episodes based on a theme. Episodic structure allows a group of students to write scenes linked thematically that can be juxtaposed to create a play. Scenes written in this way may or may not require or develop central characters and will respond to a range of stylistic conventions. Students then focus not on developing a narrative or an argument about a theme but on structuring the play to create their desired emotional experience or engagement with ideas for the audience. Scenes are structured and ordered in a way that their intensity creates meaning for audiences/spectators.

A note about open and closed structures

Playwriting, especially for young writers, is not bound by one approach to structure. As we see, episodic and linear approaches to play structure reside within a range of options available to students writing plays – comprising a spectrum of 'closed' through to 'open' including multiperspective, post-dramatic work (see Chapter 4).

For young writers, open texts are both attractive and challenging. Generating the clarity required by an audience[2] poses particular, but not insurmountable, problems for the developing writer. While 'learn the rules before you break them'

---

[2]And in many cases, the audience is a marker who only gets to read the work.

still applies, depending on the skill of the students, the lessons from post-dramatic structure may be the way to create new and invigorating theatre – even when applied to dramatic texts. This is where the teachers' dramaturg skills will be activated. Responding to the student's vision, the teacher will scaffold learning activities that enable the student to control these non-conventional techniques and to engage an audience.

A sense of an ending ...

The end of a play needs to be inevitable, but not predictable. Surprising but unavoidable. Smiley (2005) and Catron (2002) talk about plausibility and probability.

The events and resolution need to make sense within the rules of the world you create – and be prepared for, without being telegraphed. When the climax and resolution eventually arrive, we need to feel intrigued but not swindled, recognizing that things could really not have ended any other way.

My phrase for this is 'the end is in the beginning'.

This is like a reverse 'Chekhov's gun'. In the famous Chekhov's gun reference, the idea is that if you play with a gun at the beginning of a scene/play (like *Hedda Gabler*) then someone needs to be shot with it by the end. This means also that if someone is going to be shot, it's best that that moment not be the first time we see/hear of a gun. In Polly Stenham's *That Face*, the early scenes of a problematic mother–son relationship focus on dishevelled bedclothes – establishing character and mood – but in the final moments these become central to the climax of a twisted plot – symbolic and thematic. We knew that the dishevelled room was wrong – it is only at the end that we realize just how wrong.

The young writer needs to know how to hide the structure too – to guide their audience without getting caught – unless, like Brecht, they place their work in plain sight.

As with the opening pages, there is merit in focusing on the final moments. An audience should not be unsure of when to clap. At a recent production of a very good play the final moment was ruined when, as the actor delivered the curtain line, there was silence; so much that the actor had to break the moment to signal to the audience that the play was over. This was possibly a problem more with the production than with the writing, but the final moments need to 'complete' the structure, with symbol or metaphor, to signal the journey is coming to completion.

While the internal journey of the characters can be left unfinished – as with life – the audience needs to know the play has come to an end. In *That Face*, we don't need to see exactly what happens to the character Martha, but we know what the 'new balance' will look like and that we don't need or want to see any more.[3]

Structure and ideas

Using activities that play with structure as an access point for writing a play can provide the structure (pun intended) and the parameters necessary to chunk the playwriting process into manageable bites, enabling the students to take several ideas and turn them into a series of scenes.

Essentially, students use situations to build their scenes into a play.

Writing exercise: Ideas into situations

The process outlined in Chapter 6 will have students developing a premise or a guiding/organizing idea. In that chapter, I show how to use situations to create ideas for student's plays. This activity works because the situations become the structure.

---

[3]Regarding knowing when to stop, Polly Stenham suggests that if you think you can't find the end, then perhaps it has already happened and you have written past it.

In that chapter, I discuss the process of developing the idea of over-protective or helicopter parents. I asked the students, 'Where and when is the issue of overprotective parenting powerful?' Important? Life or death?

We considered the following situations:

- Two young people wanting to go to an event – party, festival, etc.
- Two parents who share different views on what is safe parenting.
- Parent and child struggling over a request to go to that party, festival, etc.
- Teens discussing the different rules they have to navigate.
- Parent(s) who allow the friends of their own child to 'drink' (for example) when they know the child's parents wouldn't approve.

What this creates is a series of scenes based on action (conflict) and the characters come from the situations. The structure is created first before characters are fleshed out or relationship's defined. The episodic nature of these scenes can develop into a linear narrative, or may stay episodic, but they provide the play's skeleton.

The following activity is a workshop that generates a series of related or even sequential situations that can form the skeleton of a play. This works with either ideas or characters and is an effective 'quick start' to a writing process.

Writing exercise: Creating situations

The workshop begins with a game of word tennis as a warm-up. This requires students, in pairs, to play a game of tennis, miming the serve and return using words instead of a ball.

A category is chosen – names, fruits, sports, countries, etc.

Students are paired and face each other across the room. One student serves the first word, miming a real tennis serve and propelling the word across to their partner, who responds by 'hitting back' and yelling out another word from that category. The tennis game continues as long as there is still energy in the room. Then, a new game begins with the other students serving and with a new category.

Ensure the categories cover the following:

- Names (male and female)
- Occupations
- Places (cities as well as locations – the zoo, the kitchen, an office, etc.)
- Objects (anything portable such as wallet, keys, necklace, umbrella, cactus, crucifix, etc.)

Then, as soon as they are finished, send students to their journals to write four lists kept in discrete columns – names, occupations, places and objects.

Only give them a few minutes or so, coaching them to keep them speed writing.

Students then randomly[4] choose one suggestion from each column and circle them. For example, the student might have circled Jane, the cellist at the zoo with a parking fine.

The students then think of a situation where these ideas all make sense. They need to justify these disparate ideas.

This stimulates the students' imagination. Ask the students to answer the following questions: Why is Jane there? Is it a meaningful location? Is Jane frightened? Who is she avoiding? Meeting? Chasing? Whose fine is it? What does it mean?

Be careful not to give them too much time to fill out a narrative – we need it to be a charged situation not a treatment for a short story.

It will generally require the student to imagine other characters, providing the potential for real and high stakes conflict.

---

[4]I choose random numbers: circle the sixth word in column A, the ninth in Column B, etc.

Students then consider all the scenes/situations that led to, and develop from, this moment in time. Is this situation the final scene? The climactic middle? The opening moment?

Students then create a list of other situations that are needed around this one and sequence the situations to create the skeleton/ structure for their story – or the sequence of scenes in their play.

Structure from the situation

A play can be structured around the rhythms of a situation.

For example, a play based around a series of *meetings* between characters – music lessons, therapy sessions, haircuts, community lectures, council/board meetings – allows for developing relationships. The playwright's ideas are framed around the context of regular but time-specific meetings and the business they involve.

Similarly, as Sweet (1993) describes, a scene or play can get its structure from *the event* that occurs in a situation: a wedding has a structure, as does a trial, which can provide the scaffold for the action.

Writing exercise: Event structure

Part 1

Write a series of scenes based around the structure provided by a wedding reception.

Before you write, complete the following chart. (I have started you off, but feel free to change or add anything that you like.)

The situation involves two key characters – A and B.

- They could be a couple or siblings or friends.
- A was once in love with the bride/groom. They broke up horribly and A is still not over it.

Event: Wedding reception	Action
Guests arrive Drinks are served	A and B arrive. A is worried that they are not dressed sexy/sophisticated/cool enough to impress ... tries to gain reassurance from B
Bride and groom arrive More drinks are served	A sees bride/groom and tries to maintain a sense of dignity by...
Meal is served	
Speeches	
Dancing	
Farewells	

Part 2

Using one of the following as a structure, write a series of scenes that follows the phases and rhythms of your chosen event: baptism, football match, school dance/prom/formal/graduation, board meeting, classroom lesson, sports carnival, trial or jury deliberation.

Write out the specific phases/moments in the event, develop some context and ensure the actions are focused.

Complete a chart similar to the one for a wedding reception above.

The scenario – why planning is important

Writing a plan before you write may help to ensure that the energy of writing is focused in a clear direction and that the playwright has a sense of where the play is going and an idea of the end point. That way, the writing can be evaluated against the goal and structured by the plan.

One approach is to write a scenario: a scene by scene breakdown of everything that happens in a play. Much like detailed backgrounds for characters, the scenario provides the skeleton for the action and dialogue, providing a map for the students to follow. Smiley (2005, p. 35) suggests that a 'writer shouldn't make the mistake of trying to write the play before thinking through the structure, even though the structure is likely to flex considerably during the drafting'. As van Itallie (1997, p. 47) suggests, a play is a journey and has a destination, so planning the route before you leave is important. You can change the route if you realize there is a better way and 'you may decide to revise the shape of your map. Your play may creatively go in directions you had not originally thought about' (p. 47).

However, the question of how much preplanning to do before you write is one hotly debated. Ibsen, for example, wrote detailed scenarios, perhaps longer than the plays themselves (see Baker, 1919), and Simon Stephens mulls over ideas, researches and plans for months before writing the play, which he then does very quickly. Other playwrights begin with writing to see where the idea will take them.[5] Wandor (2008) and Wright (1997) counsel that if preparatory work is done, writing theatrically – that is, dialogue and scenes rather than prose – will ensure the playwright creates theatrical ideas and responses to theatrical challenges.

As we saw from the quote at the beginning of the chapter, Polly Stenham believes a *flexible* scenario provides the parameters for writing dialogue, knowing she is free to be creative, free to take risks and make mistakes – and then free to rewrite – because she has an idea of where she is going.

A playwright needs something to guide them through the unknown – not too tight that you write to a formula, but not

---

[5]See Simons Stephens's National Theatre Playwrights podcast for a range of responses to the question 'Are you a planner?'.

too loose that you get lost. It can be a trail (Gooch, 2001) to a destination, a blueprint or an outline sketch, rather than a straitjacket. And how detailed this document is and what form it takes – prose, cards, images, story board – depends on the needs of the students (Itallie, 1997). Polly Stenham uses a large black wall and index cards so she can see the whole play – touch it, as she calls it.

Using a scenario responds to what we know about the iterative and recursive creative process. Writing a play is a balance between moments of insight and *long* sessions of work. The scenario is one of the ways these moments of insight can be supported by critical and imaginative thinking. The scaffold provided by a scenario allows students to make progress and to continue producing work that can be further developed and mined for new moments of insight.

Writing using a scenario allows you to access the two forms of thinking that make up creativity – critical and imaginative. It is the tension of alternating between conscious planning and inspired writing that leads to a dynamic play (Gooch, 2001, p. 64).

While planning may seem restrictive, the teaching and learning activities you create will depend on the students you have and the context in which the learning will take place. As a general suggestion, a large group with a short time in which to write will need significant scaffolding. Individuals with longer to write may be allowed to begin more freely – though careful, structured and detailed planning is still beneficial for the solo writer, making the final stages more productive. As I have said, an extra hour here can save ten at the end.

Writing exercise: Card the play

Write the whole story of your play as a narrative. This can be everything that occurs before and after the events of the play – or, if you already have a full draft, it can just be what the audience will see on stage.

Now divide the narrative into sections that might correspond to a scene – either someone leaves or enters. (If you have written the whole story, first choose the moment to begin the play and choose the moment to end and write a card for each.)

Give each scene a title (this can be as simple as 'The part where …').

Now write the title and a summary of each scene on index cards.

Place the cards in order on a table.

You can now see the whole play.

This activity is equally beneficial as a pre-writing activity as one to help with redrafting. Carding the play allows the writer to visualize the whole, lifting the structure off the page. In looking at the overall narrative structure, students can see where the end should be or when the climax needs to happen. It enables backwards engineering, placing symbols or parallel actions early in the play to set up key moments that occur later. Alternatively, this exercise can be used to understand a play that already exist. Read *Betrayal* and card the play as it occurs, numbering each scene. Then order them chronologically (this is easy – it is in reverse). Now try this for Crimps's *Attempts on Her Life*.

Writing exercise: Minimalist structure

To create the most intense play from your story, after carding your existing play, begin removing cards until the story no longer makes sense. Now replace the last card and begin to write but only using the remaining cards.

Structuring in time and shape

As a play exists as sound and sight, the length of scenes and the sounds within them need to be considered when structuring the theatrical experience.

How long are your scenes? Do they alternate between short and long? Do they lead up to a significant longer scene in the middle? Does it end sharply or with a meandering discussion of what the audience has just seen?

This is where the limitations of the stage can aid in the writing process. Like the 23-minute sit-com, writing a short play (which is likely to be the best form for a developing solo writer) or episodic work (made up of a variety of scenes written by a class) makes the playwright very conscious of shape. Scenes cannot be too brief to prevent engagement nor too long that they provide detail unsuited to the form.

Hilary Bell recalls how imposing a structure on the work helped her break through a block she was having with her play *Wolf Lullaby*. Inspired by a chance visit to a church and the stations of the cross – she thought that she might structure the play in twelve scenes. While she ultimately modified the structure further, the imposition of a structure gave her play its shape.

Writing exercises: Time and shape

For the play you are writing or have written, time each scene or count the lines/pages. Are they all the same length? Are they all brief? Are there lots of small scenes and one large one? How will that play out on stage? What experience does that provide an audience?

Represent the length of each scene graphically with boxes or shapes of differing sizes to represent stage time:

Scene 1	Scene 2	Scene 3	Scene 4	Scene 5	Scene 6	Scene 7

Now consider the intensity of the scenes. Plays, like a song/ symphony, need moments of light and shade, of building interest, of exposition, of darkness and hope, humour and tragedy. Not all of these, not in every scene of your play, but consider how light and shade might help your play.

Colour each of the boxes from cool blue (building action) to hot red (intense action). Does the structure and order of the scenes/moments create your intended journey for the audience/spectators? Remember your premise/objective. What do you want from the audience when the lights are turned back on?

As van Itallie (1997) suggests, plays 'breathe' in and out, tension and release. Audiences need moments to absorb, to cry and to laugh.

Choices need to be made about the sequence of events – it is both a generating and reducing exercise. You may need to write more scenes to set up a moment or remove scenes which spoil a reveal. Consider how much information is needed by the audience at any given moment to support a revelation or turbo charge a plot twist.

Then consider how much time an audience needs to engage with the characters and care about this climax or catastrophe. Have we seen enough of the main character to care about their obstacles? Do they need more stage time?

Structure and character knowledge

How you decide to release information applies to the characters as much as the audience. Be conscious of who knows what and when to ensure characters act on information in a plausible and probable way. Asking Hamlet to kill the King is a reveal that sustains the rest of the play – had Hamlet seen the murder, then the result would have been a much different play.

Characters will know more than each other and at times the audience needs to know more than the characters. Judging how to use the tension of dramatic irony is part of developing the skill of using structure to manage audience experience.

Writing exercise: Generating ideas with structure – climax card

Write a key climactic event on a card. Place that card on a table. Now, using as few cards as possible write all the events that need to happen before and after that event to create the experience the playwright wants for the audience.

Writing exercise: Tableaux

In a class workshop, use this tableau exercise to develop understanding of scene structure.

After a physical warm-up, ask students to form groups of three.

Give them each a word – an abstract noun such as loss, joy, betrayal, victory, etc.

Give them a short time to discuss and plan and then ask them to form a tableau that conveys that idea. Groups then present their tableaux to the class one at a time asking the other groups to identify their word from their image.

Students then are told to choose two of the other tableaux from the class to add to their own.

They then have three tableaux of abstract nouns to sequence.

Groups then devise a scene using each tableau. One becomes the beginning, another the middle and the third is the end. Students order them to create an audience journey.

The scene then transforms from the first abstract noun (say joy) moving through to another (betrayal) and ending in the third (loss). The students will begin in a freeze, then unfreeze and improvise dialogue (realistic or stylized) that moves towards the middle tableau/image; they freeze, then move and improvise more dialogue to end on the last frozen tableau.

The style of the piece depends on the interests and skill of the class, but working to enact the emotional or narrative movement required by the sequence of images emphasizes the structure of a scene. (See the apple bowl image in Figure 10.1.)

Summary

- Structure is about *how* to tell the story, *how* to reveal the information.
- Doesn't have to be linear, can be episodic/moments.
- Get in late and get out early.
- Start your play at a point of action.
- Remember to know why 'now'? Why here at this point?
- The end is in the beginning.
- Inciting incidents – what starts the play and when did it happen?
- The idea/concept chooses the form, for example *Waiting for Godot,* and form creates meaning.
- *A scenario*
  - A detailed plan of the entire play – can take many forms, but is flexible and under constant revision.
  - Map – either in prose or in diagrams – that charts the whole play to allow you to fill in the pieces.

References

Aronson, L. (2000). *Scriptwriting Updated: New and Conventional Ways of Writing for the Screen.* Crows Nest: Allen and Unwin.

Baker, G. P. (1919). *Dramatic Techniques.* London: Jonathan Cape.

Catron, L. E. (2002). *The Elements of Playwriting.* Long Grove, IL: Waveland Press, Inc.

Freytag, G. (1900). *Technique of the Drama: An Exposition of Dramatic Composition and Art* (Trans. E. J. MacEwan). Chicago: Scott, Foresman and Company.

Gooch, S. (2001). *Writing a Play.* London: A & C Black.

Grace, F. and Bailey, C. (2016). *Playwriting: A Writers' and Artists' Companion.* London and New York: Bloomsbury Academic.

Itallie, J.-C. v. (1997). *The Playwright's Workbook*. Montclair, NJ: Applause Theatre and Cinema Books.

Kaufman, M. (2001). *The Laramie Project*. New York: Vintage Books.

Smiley, S. (2005). *Playwriting: The Structure of Action*. New Haven and London: Yale University Press.

Spencer, S. (2002). *The Playwright's Guidebook*. London: Faber and Faber.

Sweet, J. (1993). *The Dramatists Toolkit: The Craft of the Working Playwright*. Portsmouth, NH: Heinemann.

Tuckett, J. (2017). 'Lesson Plan Four: Scenes'. In J. Tuckett (Ed.), *The Student Guide to Writing: Playwriting* (pp. 21–5). London: Oberon Books.

Wandor, M. (2008). *The Art of Writing Drama*. London: Bloomsbury Academic.

Wesker, A. (2010). *Wesker on Theatre*. London: Oberon Books.

Wright, M. (1997). *Playwriting in Process*. Portsmouth, NH: Heinemann.

11

Embedding symbol

Art's power is the ability to contain the idea of one thing inside something else.

TIM CROUCH (2014)

Introduction

The focus for this chapter is symbolism – the poetic in theatre.

It explores how to help students understand and control symbolism in their work. It looks at how symbol is used to complement and underscore the play's action, as well as at how verbal, aural and visual imagery can work together to deepen the audience's engagement with the ideas and moments in your play.

Symbolism elevates the play and its ideas above the reality on the stage and makes the words and images mean more than their surface or literal meaning.

As Tim Crouch (2014) suggests, some ideas carry other concepts, images and thoughts within them. The rich ambiguity allows audiences to create their own connections and their own meaning in a dramatic text.

Everything is significant ...

Unlike a novel or a poem, a play provides spectators/audiences with many sources of information simultaneously – sounds, images, dialogue, movement, character, etc. (Hayman, 1977). Audiences receive information in juxtaposition – in clusters. And those messages are transmitted in real time, without the luxury a reader has to stop and go back and reread for clarity.

When we go to the theatre we are constantly looking for clues in the performance to help us understand what the play *means* and what we can take away from the experience. And as the stage presents life 'intensified' (Burton, 2001), audiences *expect* verbal and physical symbolism and imagery. They expect things to mean more than themselves. As Burton (2001, p. 115) explains, everything – dialogue, costume, props, set, gesture, etc. – is being read for significance. Waters (2012) agrees, arguing that the qualities and, in particular, the limits of the play form place 'symbolic weight' to everything that happens on the stage. Burton (2001) even goes as far as to argue that the ability to create effective drama texts 'depends on our ability to use and understand symbol'.

An audience will make meaning from what they *see* and what they *hear*,[1] and this book consistently encourages young playwrights to write for actors moving in time and space and not disembodied voices on a page. It encourages playwrights to write with the directorial/design team in mind – giving them space to complement the play's ideas with creative input of their own. This does not mean writers direct from within. As discussed, any reference to business of production elements need to be textual not directorial.

I encourage playwrights to be focused on writing for a range of communication channels – verbal, aural, visual, temporal –

---

[1]Which is why, as Freeman (2016) suggests, it makes sense to call audiences 'spectators' as well.

to increase the power and effectiveness of their work. The teacher's job is to help the students understand and manipulate these elements, as writers select signs and symbols to control their play's poetic meaning. Understanding the power of metaphor will enable students to write plays that are dramatic and theatrical.

Symbols and the poetic

Recognizing the limitations of naturalism and its 'inadequate use of the theatre's imaginative power', Hall (2000, p. 109) calls for greater use of metaphor and the poetic to provoke our imagination (2000, p. 113).

And like poetry, symbols in drama are precise and concentrated. Through allusion and resonances, symbols create, clarify and complicate the rich meaning in a play. Symbol and motif work to strengthen and deepen the meaning, creating ambiguity that simultaneously opens and clarifies.

Symbols as a contract with the audience: The paradox of collective meaning

A play needs to be experienced and 'read' by a communal collective audience (Gooch, 2001). The playwright must understand that an audience has expectations of what a play is and a shared language of signs and symbols (Edgar, 2009, 2013).

To communicate with an audience, playwrights need to understand the semiotics of theatre: its verbal, visual and acoustic codes (Pfister, 1988). While these codes are no longer – if they ever were – thought to be homogenous, universal and singular in meaning, an audience still brings to the theatre their expectations of what 'a play' is and means. As Edgar suggests, playwrights must negotiate these expectations as they *belong* to the audience. As Freeman (2016) warns, theatre that pushes the boundaries too far is at risk of being unrecognizable to its spectators.

However, we also know that every member of the audience makes their own meaning from what they see based on their own context, knowledge and understanding of theatre. This is what Freeman (2016) calls the 1,000 subjectivities.

Playwrights write within this tension: responding to a postmodern context of subjective meaning but within a tradition of shared conventions and tropes. However, this leads to a richness, rather than a homogeneity, of theatre experience.

Writing a play is an interaction, a dialogue, with an audience. As with all communication, the symbols and images used by the playwright need to be evaluated. Ask yourself as you write, 'What signals is this play putting out?' and 'How will it be received?' (Gooch, 2001, p. 10). What kind of symbol am I using?

Three types of symbol

There are three types of symbols available to a playwright.

The first includes ideas which exist outside any specific cultural context and are universal.[2] These are ideas that *live* outside the world of theatre, such as spring and rebirth, parents and children, death and mourning, honesty and betrayal, hunger and greed.

Secondly, there are cultural symbols – of history, allegories, parables, fables and shared stories. Some of these are borrowed

---

[2] I recognize that the concept of universality is culturally complicated. I acknowledge that I am writing from a Western Anglo-Saxon tradition and yet the students we teach are from a range of cultural backgrounds that will complement and contradict many of these assumptions. This is an opportunity rather than a problem. Further, many symbolic ideas cross cultures, especially those that deal with the rituals of the seasons, animals and rhythms of life.

from other works of art and again rely on a shared cultural vocabulary. Religious motifs and allusions to other texts fall into this category. Often these may include symbols that are specific to a group and are relevant and important at a specific time. If we are writing in a Western theatre tradition the symbols may appear universal from our world view. But as cultures change, what we consider our tradition is actually dynamic and evolving.

King Lear, for example, interrogates universal ideas of love and betrayal, explored within family structures. Lear's request for a profession of love and Cordelia's 'nothing' are understood in the context of a universal empathy of the bond between parent and child. The subsequent importance of Regan and Goneril refusing to provide a home for their father evokes strong reaction (and meaning) because home is symbolically rich (and perhaps universal).

However, the specific details regarding the rules of court, or the belief in the divine right of kings, well known to the audiences of the time, will not be immediately clear to a modern audience. The symbols mean very different things, but they do mean something.

The continued relevance of Shakespeare's plays and the cross-cultural engagement with his texts suggests that there are some ideas that appeal to a wide, perhaps even universal, human audience – even if it is a theatricalized interest.

The third type of symbols are those created by the writer within the text – ideas whose relevance becomes significant as the world of the play unfolds: for example, the tree in Arthur Miller's *All My Sons*, the AIDS medicine AZT in *Angels in America* and the shared drink in *That Face*.

Symbol can work to quickly establish character and place. As Waters (2012, p. 141) suggests, drama works through synecdoche, where *parts* stand for a whole – 'a family for a nation, a tree for a forest, a room for a house'.

Many plays will contain all three, so that they sustain analysis and interpretation on a number of levels, as well as being able to generate engagement for an audience across contexts.

The following game introduces students to thinking about how complex ideas can be conveyed through symbol and allusions. It demonstrates two things: first, that people can be symbolized by an object – a car or a house can reflect and communicate personality. Secondly, that symbol carries concentrated meaning. The vehicle they chose for their play, for example, is actually the first symbolic choice they make in the playwriting process.

Writing exercise: Who am I?

Ask for a student volunteer to think of a famous person. They then tell the class one big thing about them such as 'I am a living American' or 'I am a cartoon character'.

The other students must then ask questions such as 'If you were a car, what kind of car are you?' 'What food would you be?' 'If they were a style of music what would they be?' 'If they were a style of footwear what would they be?' etc.

No direct questions. No questions that suggest a yes or no answer.

This leads to thinking in metaphors and abstractions.

Note that the question is not 'What is their favourite?' but 'What would they be?' The idea is to imagine the person in another form which creates metaphor and symbol.

Communicating symbols

As we said, a symbol is something that represents itself and something else. There are several ways to communicate these layers of ideas to an audience. As Waters (2012) suggests:

1   Verbal symbols create images in the mind of the audience.

2 Visual symbols create imagery and *connections* that complement, extend or contradict the verbal images the audience hears.

3 Aural/sound imagery conveys information and creates mood.

And symbols are created by:

a words
b gesture
c sounds
d setting
e objects/props
f theatrical elements of set and lighting, sfx, etc.

Verbal symbols

Words create images in the mind of the audience/spectators. This aural poetry uses many common poetic devices, such as simile, metaphor, allusion and analogy. For instance, the dialogue chapter explored how *what* is said can, and in most cases should, have more than one level of meaning. In a good play, a character's dialogue needs to resonate beyond the world on the stage, perhaps even beyond the time of the performance. Dialogue, even though it is primarily one character's 'actions' on another, will make use of allusions and poetic devices to make meaning for an audience.

Audience engagement is enhanced by moments of realization. In *That Face,* the audience realizes that Martha asking Henry to drink with her is certainly an action – but is also a symbol of her wanting him to show his love and allegiance for her. Verbal imagery can direct the audience to the key issues – the 'aha' moment when we realize we are no longer talking about a roof over our head (Lear), a celebratory drink (*That Face*) or the tree (*All My Sons*).

With verbal imagery, repetition is often needed to underline the idea for the audience. Gooch (2001) uses the metaphor of spinning plates: that playwrights need to revisit a symbol or metaphor every now and then to keep it in the air, to keep it in the audience's minds so they don't wonder what happened to it. Shakespeare's disease images in *Hamlet* and Stoppard's references to the limits of the stage in *Rosencrantz and Guildenstern Are Dead* remind the audience that these plays are doing more than just telling a story.

Therefore, a recurring line, phrase or concept will take on symbolic meaning – whether intended or not – and a repeated idea without symbol will be read as lazy.

Writing exercise: Poetic monologue

Write a monologue for one of your characters (from your play or one you create for this exercise) where they describe a defining moment from their childhood – a key event that has affected them and impacts upon their relationships in the present.

Reread the monologue and decide upon the action. You need to choose who they are telling it to and their relationship, etc. What object or event features in the story? Is it a toy lost on a holiday? Or a parent who missed a dance performance?

Why is this story important now? Why are they telling this person and what does it mean to them? Is it to justify, apologize, convince, etc. How do the details of the earlier event impact on the events of today? What parallels or allusions are important? Is it a parable?

Write a second draft. Develop the key details of the event to emphasize the symbolic aspect of this action, object or event – the past events now stand for something else. Try to create that 'aha' moment in the audience where they now know that you are no longer just talking about the dance perfomance or the toy.

Writing exercise: Unimportant objects, serious fights

Write a short scene where your characters, A and B, a couple, are brushing their teeth.

They begin to quarrel over the toothpaste, but it becomes clear the aspects of the paste – its flavour, its cost, the cap not being put back on – are symbols for aspects of their relationship. Perhaps there are money issues and they can no longer afford this luxury toothpaste; or perhaps the cap being left off is an act of defiance.

Choose what they are fighting over – infidelity, finances, freedom.

Write the scene where by the end the audience knows why they are fighting but the actual underlying cause of the fight is *never* mentioned.

Writing exercise: Backpack revisited

Remember the imaginary backpack/handbag you created for one of your characters? Revisit these items turning up the symbolism. Rethink the pack, and choose items that will become central props for these characters that complement, reflect and therefore symbolize their personalities, contradictions and/or wants. These items will be essential to their character business or even the plot of the play. In other words, they must feature in the action of the scene/play – not just convey character.

Choose one of the items, and write a scene where the chosen item features. The character needs to use it or lose it or give it away or replace it – all of which results in significant consequences for the action of the scene/play. Think Hedda Gabler and the pistols.

The consequences need to be greater than the 'worth' of the object would suggest. (This is device used with devastating results in *Othello* with regard to Desdemona's handkerchief.)

Character and symbolic gesture

Character gestures become symbolic when they complement, contradict or extend the ideas in the text – often unconsciously revealing the characters real thoughts, flaws or motivations. For example, a character who disinfects his hands after shaking hands when he meets people signifies obsessive behaviour, arrogance or guilt. It also taps into the universal idea of 'washing your hands' of a situation and the concept of dirty hands meaning complicity. There is great scope for this gesture to create symbolic undertones that enrich the text with meaning for the audience to 'create'. Lady Macbeth's hand wringing is layered – the *real* blood on her hands could not be removed by soap and water.

When I was young, I always knew that we were in trouble if my father whistled as he loudly washed the dishes. No words necessary!

These gestures work best in cluster. Think about how all the bits of information are read and thus several subtle moments will cluster together and build a symbolic environment – rather than just choosing one big symbol that might offend the intelligence of the audience. You don't need to call the antagonist Dr Evil.

Writing exercise: Symbolic stage business

Choose two characters: A and B. They are in a mutual comfortable environment: their home/office/work, etc.

A wants B to do something – leave, apologize, ask them out, do the dishes, etc.

As they converse about the events of the day/details of work, A is completing a physical action – washing the dishes/shredding documents. The intensity of the activity increases as A feels they are not being listened to. As they get closer to their goal, they become calmer.

Improvise/write the scene using dialogue and specific stage directions. Create vivid stage actions and character gestures to symbolize the subtext. The scene ends when A succeeds or gives up. The focus is using physical activity to symbolize their emotional state or the subtext of the conversation.

Visual symbols: Setting

The first image a playwright creates and, therefore, the first symbols seen by the play's audience are contained in the setting and the *set* description, realized by the designers and crew. As Catron (2002) suggests, visual elements create the universe of the play. A successful stage world will represent far more than the specific time and place (Grace and Bailey, 2016). It needs to suggest a range of realities.

The set tells the audience where they are – but also specifies what *kind* of where – stylistically and thematically. While often very sparsely described, the setting of a play can make use of all levels of symbol – universal, cultural and those unique to the play. The description of the set can include symbols of place and time and will include clues about style. It will set up expectations in the audience about what kind of play they will see and 'how' they are supposed to read it.

The audience will read the world of the play is a microcosm for society at large. In *Betrayal*, the world of publishing and bourgeois manners is allegorical, representing something about all people and all relationships. The conscious literary world within the fictional world – the characters in the play are talking about a novel about betrayal – highlights the impact of art on life.

The onstage world might mirror our world or contradict it. Highlighting contrasts between the world outside the play and the world onstage is an effective way to underline meaning. Louis Nowra's *The Golden Age* contains several 'worlds' that, in juxtaposition, create significant symbolic meaning. The play opens in suburban pre-Second World War Tasmania, Australia, made unusual by the inclusion of a crumbling pair of Greek columns that we quickly identify as a set for Euripides's play *Iphigenia in Taurus*. The 'world' within a world metaphor is emphasized when a long-lost decaying tribe, descended from escaped convicts, is discovered in the depths of the Tasmanian wilderness. They are returned to civilization, creating scenes of metaphoric time travel and language barriers. These worlds are juxtaposed further with the inclusion of both a battlefield in war-torn Germany and then a prison in a post-war world. This play explores the ideas of civilization and cultural assumptions and creates much of this meaning through the audience creating meaning in the juxtapositions – complementing the plot and characterization.

How these ideas are realized is the role of the director – your setting gives the production team something to develop. Importantly, any props that are used will need to mean more than their apparent/superficial function (unless they are context-making – sometimes characters are just making a cup of tea).

To explore these ideas, the symbol of the broken apple tree in Arthur Miller's *All My Sons* warrants some detailed discussion. Much like the plays of Ibsen, the inciting incident that creates the action of the play occurred many years before the start of the play and the suffering we see is a result of one of the character's earlier mistakes.

The play begins with detailed stage directions that create a sense of 'seclusion' – a backyard surrounded by fences. The stage directions create a specific picture with backyard furniture, etc. – functional but vivid.

Central to the meaning of the play – not immediately known of course – is a description of a tree. Representing the missing dead son, it becomes a powerful reminder and manifestation of his presence throughout the play. And, as a tree takes a while to grow, the concept of time is embedded in the symbol.

The precision of the stage directions for the tree – including placement on stage, size and even that there is fruit still attached despite being toppled over – tells a director and the audience specific things. With concentrated energy, the playwright connects the memory of the son with this 'broken' tree. Broken by a storm the previous night (answering the 'why now' question), the tree that still has fruit clinging to it, symbolizing his youth and unfulfilled promise, is the focus of his mother's attempt to keep his memory alive.

At the beginning of Act 2, there are two key moments where the characters' interactions with the 'tree' (which the audience reads as the brother) create engaging and layered dramatic meaning. As the act begins, Chris Keller, the brother of the deceased Larry, saws the broken tree free from the stump and removes it from the stage. The audience reads this as Chris's attempt to free his family (and himself) from the oppressive memory of his brother. When left alone on stage, Ann, the missing/dead son's ex and the living son Chris's current fiancé, reveals her emotional and mental state: alone on the stage, Ann walks to the tree stump and lovingly but hesitantly touches the top of the stump. In these actions, we see the tree as a vivid symbol of the brother's presence and the fragility of the present relationships. These key stage moments are iconic images that remain in the audiences memory and come to sum up the wider action (Waters, 2012).

Stage pictures

Like the tableaux exercises we use in a drama class, manipulating *mise en scene* evokes feelings and responses from an audience; again, while we are not writing in directions writers still need to be aware that we are writing spatially.

- What images are you creating for your spectators?
- Who is on stage?
- What props are on stage?
- What symbols do these create/enable/activate?

The final situation for Brecht's Mother Courage – left alone, walking aimlessly with her cart – provides great scope for a symbolic moment using sound and visual imagery to represent more than just the end of this play.

The Australian play *7 Stages of Grieving,* by Wesley Enoch and Deborah Mailman, begins by creating a vivid and symbolic *experience* for the audience – utilizing visual, aural and even olfactory 'signs' to place the audience in a *world*. The sound of dripping ice, the smell of burning eucalyptus and the wailing of an unknown woman greet the audience as they enter the space. The set is black dirt contained by a border of white. Each element suggests more than its literal meaning, especially to an Australian audience.

Throughout the course of the play, the Indigenous actress, wearing a white dress, becomes more and more blackened by the dirt of the set. And as the performance unfolds, the props of each scene are left on stage – leaving us with a cluttered 'mess' representing the state of Indigenous – European relations in Australia.

Props are chosen consciously and are text, not decoration. They can convey character, theme, mood, action, etc. Writers incorporate these physical elements when they bring complementary meaning. With the technological advances that have made the more-than-a-century-old use of projections in theatre even easier to incorporate, the scope for the playwright to incorporate image as text, as visual poetry, is ever increasing. For example, the Sydney Theatre Company's 2016 production of Angela Betzien's *The Hanging* used projected images of bushland to create the feeling of isolation in the scene and to represent the place where the missing girls at the centre of the play had disappeared.

Writing exercise: Stage directions as symbols

Choose a scene you have written for your play or one you have completed for an exercise in this book. Search for images (photos, paintings, etc.) that might provide context or complementary theatricality to your words.

Now, focus on moments in the scene – the movements, the game, the struggle, the plot point even – and find images that complement them. Create a slideshow that plays behind the scene as you read it – a visual equivalent of a soundtrack. Consider what this brings to your play.

Introducing symbols to your text

An activity Hilary Bell suggests in her classes is to actively try to find a line of dialogue in your scenes that can be replaced by a piece of business. When considering the symbolic and poetic world of your play, think of what information or meaning can be conveyed by symbols or signs. Consider what can be signified and alluded to without having to be 'stated'.

Writing exercise: Symbols chart

The following chart explores how you can use signs and symbols to convey both text and subtext.

The idea on the left, whether it be location or time, is the information you wish to convey, and the performance codes on the right are ways a writer can use symbol and signs to convey that information more intensely (showing not telling). It shows and how signs can underline subtext or recurring parallels by create juxtaposing images.

Remember, references to set, costume or props must be text – the football jersey is a symbol of character, the gun must be used. They are not decorations. Anything not essential to character or plot is not text, but the writer doing the director or designers' jobs.

Information to 'show' to an audience	Performance sign or symbol that will communicate this to an audience = text	Examples
The where of the 'world', of the story its culture/society/ location/setting	Set – Props, Costume, etc. Visual images of the world, Aural = accents/ sound signifiers Music/SFX	*7 Stages of Grieving* – the large tree, black dirt and circle of white Period costume/uniforms and swords in productions of Shakespeare Backdrop of the bushland in Betzien's *The Hanging* Irish accents in *Lieutenant of Inishmore* The sound of cicadas places the play in the Australian summer. Sirens indicate urban environments.
When = Signalling historical moment(s) The duration of the story: time shifts structure	Set Costume Set changes, etc. lighting costume change blackout = scene changes music as transitions Music to convey historical time time-specific sounds/SFX	Historical – Ibsen's *A Doll's House* (perhaps) Brecht's *Mother Courage* The set of *The Present* in Act 2 after the explosion – from realistic to surrealistic white (as found in the STC Production Sunrise/sunset through lighting (e.g. *Hedda Gabler*) Juxtapose period and modern costumes to show different times on the same set – for example *Arcadia*. Mood creating /defining 1980s soundtracks versus classical music versus punk music versus jazz, etc. Alarm clocks/church bells

Information to 'show' to an audience	Performance sign or symbol that will communicate this to an audience = text	Examples
Who = characters relationships/ hierarchy	Dialogue and non-verbal utterances Costume, etc. Visual signs/gesture Props Proxemics set motif/symbols	Accents/quirks of syntax to show class, emotional state, etc. Biff's football jersey in *Death of a Salesman* Macheath's gloves Walking stick conveys frailty – or pretention Status shown by standing or sitting when they should or shouldn't, etc. Status or intimacy reflected in the set – bedroom/ boardroom/office, etc.

Adapted from Taylor (2002).

Read through the chart and think of ways you can introduce symbols to the scenes you have written. Think of how you can develop a character through props – how they read the paper, clean the house, etc. Or explore a theme through a symbolic action. Consider the situation where a partner wishes their spouse would buy them flowers and places an empty vase in the middle of the table each morning. What happens when the spouse finally brings home a bunch of roses, only to find the empty vase that was central to the set the whole time is now gone – perhaps even broken in the bin?

The idea is that if someone sends a letter, it must do more than convey information; it must also symbolize the end of a relationship (the letter contains a confession) or the end of a life (it contains a denial of a pardon). It can even be a sign of freedom (a resignation) but it must stand for something else.

Reread your scenes and see if you can introduce a symbol – and remove a line of dialogue – to take the scene further.

Symbolic titles: 'Crunching it down'

As a teacher, I have supervised and taught many students writing plays for external assessment – major projects with their senior studies in drama and English.

One of these students wrote a play about her Chinese-Australian heritage. She was stuck on finding a way to represent or symbolize the clash of cultures so central to her play. In discussion, she began to tell stories of what it was like growing up as a child of two cultures. She spoke of her loving grandmother who wanted her to keep her Chinese identity and gave her Chinese lanterns as presents – many, many Chinese lanterns. She laughed that her wardrobe was full of them.

When asked to symbolize her Australian life, she stumbled on the image of a Hill's hoist – a backyard clothes line that features in many suburban backyards in Australia.

Then she spoke of family Christmases where there were always two tables of food – one with food prepared by her Chinese family and one with food for her 'Australian' relatives.

The discussion continued. As the objective is to *make theatre*, these stories, images and objects were amalgamated to make the central stage picture, which also ended up being the title of the play. The play was called *Lantern on a Wire* and the bulk of the action takes place in the backyard around a celebration. There are tables of food on either side of a Hill's hoist that has been decorated with Chinese lanterns.

The central metaphor, encapsulated in the title, created a clear visual for the audience to access the play's world and its meaning.

Summary

- An audience will read everything as significant, so choose carefully.
- Theatre is best when it is poetic.

- Symbols are words, actions, sounds, objects that have resonances that go beyond their literal meaning.
- There are visual, aural and verbal symbols.
- Dialogue creates symbols through poetic devices of allusion, metaphor and analogy.
- The world, created by the setting, conveys the rules of the play the audience will be seeing.
- Stage directions create visual symbols that can complement, contrast or extend the ideas provided by plot and characterization.

References

Burton, B. (2001). *Living Drama*. Sydney, Melbourne, Brisbane, Perth: Longman.

Catron, L. E. (2002). *The Elements of Playwriting*. Long Grove, IL: Waveland Press, Inc.

Crouch, T. (2014). 'Theatre and Reality and Avoiding the Stage's Kiss of Death'. *The Guardian*, 18 June. Retrieved from https://www.theguardian.com/stage/2014/jun/18/theatre-reality-adler-and-gibb-tim-crouch-playwright

Edgar, D. (2009). *How Plays Work*. London: Nick Hern Books.

Edgar, D. (2013). 'Playwriting Studies: Twenty Years On'. *Contemporary Theatre Review*, 23(2), 99–106. doi:10.1080/10486801.2013.777056.

Freeman, J. (2016). *New Performance/New Writing*. London: Palgrave Macmillan.

Gooch, S. (2001). *Writing a Play*. London: A & C Black.

Grace, F. and Bailey, C. (2016). *Playwriting: A Writers' and Artists' Companion*. London and New York: Bloomsbury Academic.

Hall, P. (2000). *Exposed by the Mask: Form and Language in Drama*. London: Oberon Books.

Hayman, R. (1977). *How to Read a Play*. London: Eyre Methuen.

Pfister, M. (1988). *The Theory and Analysis of Drama*. Cambridge: Cambridge University Press.

Taylor, V. (2002). *Stage Writing*. Ramsbury (England): Crowood Press.

Waters, S. (2012). *The Secret Life of Plays*. London: Nick Hern Books.

12

Page to stage

I think, having a [workshop] reading is quite a lot of pressure – and when you are casting a reading and you know you are going to have to sit and hear it and have these fab actors do it – and it is going to be immensely useful– there is a degree of pride that kicks in and ego which I think can be quite motivating, actually.

POLLY STENHAM

Introduction

While teaching with, for and about creativity are considered essential for twenty-first-century education (Craft, 2011), there is often very little practical advice for teachers wanting to ensure that happens. Chapter 3, 'Creativity and Engagement', explored how the process of writing a play involves phases of imaginative and evaluative work. This chapter covers the process of bringing the numerous drafts of a play to a standard ready for performance or submission for assessment.

However, the focus of this chapter is not on rewriting, as that is part of the recursive process covered in each chapter, but on collaboration, such as workshops and readings, and how creative collaboration in the classroom can be acknowledged, utilized and harnessed.

The chapter explores how, by using collaboration to offer generative rather than limiting feedback, students' imaginative energy is enhanced and their ability to evaluate their own work is increased.

Creativity and collaboration

Drama and theatre are collaborative arts – in creation and in performance. Theatre is co-created, employing rehearsals and workshops to gather multiple perspectives – actor, director and audience – to identify opportunities in the text and generate performance.

Collaboration is a key technique for creativity teaching. Drama teachers are well-versed in using collaboration for group performance – devised or scripted. However, the benefits of collaboration for creativity are often overlooked when students are working on individual tasks. Teachers may consider that the pressures of assessment and monitoring individual progress make using collaboration in individual tasks problematic. This chapter explores how teachers can navigate these issues and use creative collaboration with their students in writing a play.

As discussed in Chapter 3, collaboration is essential to creativity. As Csikszentmihalyi argues, creativity is enriched by diversity, and centres of creativity have historically occurred at the 'intersection of different cultures, where beliefs, lifestyles and knowledge mingle and allow individuals to see new combinations of ideas with greater ease' (Csikszentmihalyi, 1996, p. 8).

Students interact and collaborate with the ideas of others, improvising within their cultural context and refusing to abide by the limits of aesthetic traditions (Gattenhof, 2006, p. 13). Young people experience and engage with creative processes and products through redactive creativity (Haseman, 2012) involving the 'skillful editing together [of] a range of materials from a wide range of sources and contexts to create the final form' (Haseman, 2012, p. 26). Creativity in the modern classroom is characterized by collaborative idea sharing, unbound by aesthetic conventions and resembling postmodern bricolage. As Vygotsky (2004) suggests, the concept of a sole author of a creative process or product ignores the true collective nature of the phenomenon. Collaboration also accesses the playfulness necessary to creativity. Vygotsky argues that 'drama more than any other form of creation is closely and directly linked to play, which is the root of all creativity in children' (2004, p. 70).

Creative environments

For Vygotsky (2004, p. 30), the environment has a significant impact on creativity, both as a catalyst and by providing the conditions necessary for it to thrive. Jefferson and Anderson (2017) suggest that for collaboration to flourish, a teacher needs to create a classroom environment of trusting relationships, valuing others and working towards a joint venture. I suggest that this 'joint venture' can be framed as group success and academic achievement, rather than the usual competitiveness that surrounds individual performance. In this way, students compete with the task and not each other.

Teachers need to encourage student collaboration and to expect, support, model and reward creativity when it is displayed (Sternberg, 2010, p. 402). Specifically, teachers can encourage creativity by creating a climate that values the questioning of assumptions, sensible risk taking and tolerance of ambiguity (Sternberg, 2010). Using Isaksen and Ekvall's (2010) creative climate model as a lens, creative collaboration can be encouraged by attending to key aspects of classroom environment. They argue that creativity needs to be supported by creating environments that are playful and that provide opportunities for imaginative idea-time, allowing a sense of fun and spontaneity. The environment will support creative development by encouraging constructive debate that values different perspectives and different points of view. This will also mean that conflict is minimized, and a climate of social and emotional safety and trust is established. It will also encourage a willingness to take sensible risks and not be afraid to make mistakes. The sense of play, trust and willingness to make mistakes will encourage students' creative capacity and confidence.

The environment for creativity requires the acceptance of the paradox of error; that mistakes are necessary and are to be evaluated and harvested for positive information (Tahirsylaj, 2012). Intelligent fast fail (Tahirsylaj, 2012) reinforces how positive responses to failures and evaluation of errors can improve creative capacity and creative confidence. Many of these ideas, such as willingness to make and share errors, collaboration of ideas and playfulness, are difficult to encourage in a classroom where individual progress needs to be identified and measured. But a classroom environment of collaboration can 'expand the potential creativity of what individuals can achieve alone' (Jefferson and Anderson, 2017, p. 135).

Creativity workshop

Students' idea generation is aided by collaboration – talking through their thoughts with trusted others. This allows the students to discover exactly what they think and what further ideas they generate in others.

As such, collaboration can begin before there are drafts or examples of product. Sharing drafts probably shouldn't be the first time students seek collaborative input.

Collaboration needs rules and must be introduced clearly and with defined boundaries. It is easy to critique an unfinished work but harder to look for the possibilities – harder to look for the gold.

Writing exercise: Workshop for idea generation

In this *formal* collaborative classroom exercise, students share their creative progress. Initially it can be the beginnings of their idea – a world, an image, a 'line of inquiry' that inspires them, or it can be a character or a scene they talk through.

Later, it may be a scene they want to share in a workshop reading, looking to create new ideas. However, no first drafts are read.

When one student offers their ideas, other students will listen and/or observe. This can be in groups or a whole class depending on time and the context. (Alternatively, students can create a display/ideas wall, where others can walk around, interact at their own pace and offer feedback in written form (monitored by the teacher).)

They then give feedback, in a spirit of generosity and intellectual play, that explores the possibilities and connections the students see in the work.

Students respond in a number of ways. They can discuss:

- Ideas in the piece that inspire them to want to know more: Who was that character? What was that idea? Where will they/that idea go?
- Ideas that inspire new or imaginative thoughts in them: 'When you said "x" it made me think of "y"' or 'that makes me think about memories of my youth or fears for the future or an interaction I had on the train'.
- Ideas that spark in them – images, texts (allusions or inspirations) links to existing art or phenomena.

It is about accessing the group's corporate knowledge – collaborative sharing to encourage possibility thinking and to spark new ideas in the playwright. It is about getting feedback on the meaning and power of your choices and understanding the effect of your ideas on others, i.e. audience response. These discussions are generative and generous – not evaluative or judgemental. Students are not to use the words *good* or *bad* or *I liked this* or *I didn't like that* – they are not to assess.

They consider: What ideas inspired or energized them? What ideas have 'legs'? The responses are judged by the ideas it sparks – and by the playwright – not the audience.

Students are not to tell others how *they* would complete the task, but share ideas that the work inspires, generates or suggests. It is an interaction with the ideas and aspects of the work that the student observer responds to positively. It is also not collaborative problematization: 'What I think is wrong is …'. It aims to *find the gold* that perhaps the student playwright has missed, or undervalued.

This collaboration, regulated by the teacher, would allow students to increase the quantity and diversity, even complexity, of their ideas, increasing the students' creative capacity.

This creative collaboration, sharing their work with others and gaining both informative and affirming feedback, can be a positive and energizing force in students' writing process and is too significant an experience to ignore.[1]

Playwriting: Collaboration and feedback

Teaching playwriting is a rich form of creative pedagogy. Students will respond most creatively in environments that include collaboration with others, a focus on play and learning from mistakes. In practice this usually and correctly means that playwriting students will benefit from feedback from a number of 'sounding boards'.

Feedback from a multiplicity of voices, provided by workshop readings, can provide both an audience response

---

[1] In my study, for many of the students, idea-sharing formed the most memorable and enjoyable aspect of the experience.

and creative idea-sharing. While, due to time constraints, it may seem impractical or even impossible to have a full reading, the benefits of some form of staged or moved reading are significant.

First, the students see staged readings as essential to them understanding the meaning of their play. They 'see' the effectiveness of their writing for performance, in time and space. They see their characters, hear the dialogue and see what their stage directions communicate to others – even if it is a pretend director.

This workshop gives student playwrights an insight into their own work. As if 'reading' it from a new perspective, the workshop creates a distancing device to allow the students to stand outside their work and evaluate it. It gathers responses from multiple perspectives to help the students understand the effect of their signs and symbols.

The embodied presence of the actors on stage provides students with another form of collaborative idea development. The actors' performance highlights ideas for the playwright to develop and generates new ideas for them to pursue. It highlights aspects that are working and can suggest new areas to focus upon or develop. The way an actor performs a character, the way the words sound together, creates new ideas, new possibilities to spark further ideas. Having actors embody and play the characters makes their interactions, actions and relationships clear. Actors' choices with the material also create opportunities for the playwright to collaborate with the performers in the writing of the play. And early embodiment allows students to see any fundamental problems before they become too committed to an unworkable idea or concept. In other words – off the page and on the stage as quickly as possible.

Positive and constructive feedback allows the playwright to get an idea of the effectiveness of the work, but also to hear reactions that can be incorporated into the play. In my study, a student reacted to an interpretation of her work by admitting that, while the ideas offered by her classmate were not her intention, she would incorporate them in her next draft.

While this is of clear benefit early in the process it is just as important in later stages of writing, where these ideas allow precise rewriting and polishing. The performance demonstrates the text's strengths, including the accuracy of the dialogue, as well as the overall style of the writing and whether the writer has communicated her objectives.

These collaborative activities are meaning-making events for the playwright and actors/readers. Collaboration with peers generates possibilities and provides emotional support to the usually isolated writer.

To enable peer feedback, the creativity workshop and readings develop ideas rather than just assess the play, making a distinction between assessment feedback and process feedback. The reading, detached from assessment, allows students to be forthcoming in telling the writer what they took from the play and allowing the writer to decide whether it works. This collaboration allows the teacher to stand back from assessing too. Teachers can allow the workshop to focus the writer on the ideas that needed clarification, using audience feedback to provide a new perspective on the play's theatrical meaning. This stepping back and allowing the student to hear from others addresses the student–mentor power imbalance. A collaborative approach works to empower the student and, while it cannot remove the uneven relationship, as discussed in Chapter 5, it repositions the teacher as one who helps the student respond to feedback rather than the critic who tells them what is wrong. Collaboration and multiple sounding boards encourage the student to not always give priority to their teacher's views, which is actually a benefit to objective assessment and monitoring of student progress.

Collaborative readings can be learning events for writer and readers. In a play-reading session for one of the students in my research, the student actors and audience, through discussing the internal processes involved in acting and responding to the play, informed the playwright of the effectiveness of their words and signs. One student asked, 'Can I take a stab at what it means?' and proceeded to analyse the script from 'within', as an actor, creating meaning unknown to the student playwright. The student playwright responded, 'No, [that's not what I meant] but I can see where you could get that', and then proceeded to explain her intended meaning. The readers demonstrated the strengths shown in performance. Another student in my study found that the involvement of the actors highlighted ideas to develop and generated new ideas to pursue. The feedback provided by the embodiment of their play in the staged readings lead to major rewrites for several of the students.

After the workshop, the student playwrights emphasized how validating a reading can be, providing them with insights into their own work. For one, it helped clarify structure, as she was able to see the entirety of her text and the impact of pacing and scene length on audience engagement. Others were able to see the impact of characters and their relationships – seeing them interact on the floor – and realized that one of her characters who, on the page, she intended to be a 'side character' was, on the stage, endearing and meaningful for the audience.

Some caveats

This process needs to be clearly set up, with the students being given opportunities to practice collaborative feedback in class in low stakes situations. Students should develop their collaborative creativity and idea-sharing during normal drama class improvisations and workshop devising, so they can learn the skills of possibility feedback (rather than problematizing) as they engage with devising work in junior classes and non-assessable performances in senior drama workshops.

Due to the personal nature of playwriting, collaborative feedback can be met with resistance if it is perceived as *criticism*. The higher the stakes of the assessment, the more students will be reluctant to play, fearing their ideas may be diluted or 'stolen'. Students will fear losing control. If properly facilitated, this process can give more control to the student. While their ideas are shared, they still take on only what they want and modify, synthesise and create new ideas that will transform and develop their work far beyond the ideas offered in the workshop.

The collaborative teaching and learning environment positions input as generative rather than critical. Students need to see it as a resource not a correction. Collaborative input should protect and yet develop the student's initial or core vision. The risk with collaboration is that if the student has insufficient domain knowledge to inform their judgements, input from others can be destabilizing rather than liberating. Workshop feedback, then, may not necessarily result in improved writing. Collaborative feedback is beneficial, perhaps even necessary, but it is not sufficient to writing a good play.

Another caveat is the danger of making choices based on *popularity*. Collaborative feedback is not surrendering responsibility for choices to a focus group. The process is part of a process that involves significant skill development and understanding of playwriting to allow students to judge the merit of the play themselves and not to *rely* on the opinions of others.

The classroom environment that develops, rewards and expects creativity encourages the sharing and generating of ideas with playfulness, trust and open debate (Isaksen and Ekvall, 2010). As a classroom strategy, the staged reading creates such an environment. The moved reading allows the student to see what is and is not working and can receive feedback from the audience and the teacher. Further, using performances or staged readings solely as assessment limits its usefulness for idea creation or clarification and focuses on the teacher and audience as evaluator.

The environment for creativity will be one that values students' ideas – both their original work and other students' comments on it. It will encourage risk taking, both with ideas and form, but within the context of highly developed skills and understanding of the task and what is expected of them. The workshop approach to creative problem finding and idea generation would be applicable to a range of contexts, with students engaging with the work of others, responding to sparks of inspiration and envisaging innovative combinations that generate further creative energy for the process (Sawyer, 2012). The potential improvement to classroom creativity and engagement from embracing collaborative practice has implications across other aspects of drama, arts and education in general.

The individual creator is supported by the collaborative community, with the specific ideas being incorporated as little or as much as the individual student decides. The students' shared vision, the joint venture (Jefferson and Anderson, 2017), is mutual learning and development. While easier in a context of external (rather than internal) competition, it is not impossible. Further, this is not co-writing, but a co-creation of meaning.

Building collaboration into the creative process utilizes the benefits of the energy and cross fertilization of ideas. And the earlier teachers do it, the more fertile and inspirational (rather than unsettling) this sharing can be. As Sawyer (2012) argues, the process is one of many sparks of inspiration: the more energized the process, the more ideas can be generated, combined and evaluated (Isaksen and Ekvall, 2010).

Collaboration of ideas is similarly not a panacea. It needs to be supported by knowledge of the creative process (Sawyer, 2012) to inform students of 'how' collaboration fits into their vision as well as creating a climate based on trust, idea support, rigorous debate (Isaksen and Ekvall, 2010) and significant domain knowledge (Csikszentmihalyi, 1996). Students need to *understand* the process of creativity to enable a confident collaborative approach. Risk taking (Isaksen and Ekvall, 2010) and embracing of mistakes (Tahirsylaj, 2012) are part of the creative process.

The lessons from the drama room suggest that greater understanding of creativity will increase the benefits of collaboration. Building an environment that encourages, rewards and expects creative sharing will benefit teachers and students and prepare both for the demands of the twenty-first-century classroom and workplace.

Summary

- Drama and theatre are collaborative arts – in creation and in performance.
- Collaboration is essential for creativity and is a key technique for creativity teaching.
- Creative collaboration in the classroom is to be acknowledged, utilized and harnessed.
- Teachers can ensure their classroom climates support and foster creativity.
- When collaboration offers generative rather than limiting feedback, students' imaginative energy is enhanced and their ability to evaluate their own work is increased.
- Students will be more able to develop their creativity in a classroom that understands the benefits of failure.
- Teachers can establish collaborative strategies and practices that generate creative ideas and reward and develop students' individual creativity.
- Collaborative play readings enable students to gather a rich variety of sources of feedback. They create an evaluative distance that empowers their own dramaturgical understanding and diminishes the role of teacher as critic.

- Collaboration is a process – not a silver bullet. Skill and knowledge are still key to playwriting proficiency.

References

Craft, A. (2011). *Creativity and Education Futures: Learning in a Digital Age*. Stoke on Trent, UK and Sterling USA: Trentham Books.

Csikszentmihalyi, M. (1996). *Creativity: Flow and the Psychology of Discovery and Invention*. New York: Harper Collins.

Gattenhof, S. (2006). *Drivers of Change: Contemporary Australian Theatre for Young People*. City East, QLD: Drama Australia.

Haseman, B. (2012). 'Old and New Arguments for Placing Drama at the Centre of the Curriculum'. *Drama Queensland Says*, 35(1), 24–35.

Isaksen, S. G. and Ekvall, G. (2010). 'Managing for Innovation: The Two Faces of Tension in Creative Climates'. *Creativity and Innovation Management*, 19(2), 73–88.

Jefferson, M. and Anderson, M. (2017). *Transforming Schools: Creativity, Critical Reflection, Communication, Collaboration*. London and New York: Bloomsbury Academic.

Sawyer, R. K. (2012). *Explaining Creativity: The Science of Human Innovation*. Oxford and New York: Oxford University Press.

Sternberg, R. J. (2010). 'Teaching for Creativity'. In R. A. Berghetto and J. C. Kaufman (Eds), *Nurturing Creativity in the Classroom* (pp. 394–414). Cambridge and New York: Cambridge University Press.

Tahirsylaj, A. S. (2012). 'Stimulating Creativity and Innovation Through Intelligent Fast Failure'. *Thinking Skills and Creativity*, 7(3), 265–70.

Vygotsky, L. S. (2004). 'Imagination and Creativity in Childhood'. *Journal of Russian and East European Psychology*, 42(1), 7–97.

13

Conclusion

*Playwriting is very personal and there are so many
different ways to write a play. And I don't presume
to have 'the' answers. And the way that I write a
play and the methods that I feel I can impart may
not be right for everybody.*

VANESSA BATES (PLAYWRIGHT)

The objective of this book is to provide ideas and a range of
activities to demystify the teaching of playwriting. It aims to
provide teachers with resources for their own professional
learning and to enable them to scaffold the teaching and
learning experience for their students. While it provides
parameters, the approach is broad and provocative, rather
than prescriptive and narrow.

This, I am sure, has led to contradictions within the
book – suggestions that seem at odds with ideas expressed
elsewhere. In some ways, I hope that has been the case. To
respond to the variety of teachers and students who will
turn to this book as a resource, the catholicity of views
is something I embrace and hope, as teachers, you do as
well. Even the most accomplished playwright can only tell
you what works for them. I have adopted a dramaturgical
approach and asked you as educators to choose the ideas

and strategies that work best for you, in your context and with your students.

And as with most drama activities, these tasks and exercises are open, allowing students to complete them to the best of their ability at this particular moment in their development. Each exercise can be repeated by the same student months apart and reap very different results, and still bring out the best in all students – middle school to graduate students.

Developing greater playwriting proficiency in schools will work to broaden the skills base of our young writers and encourage diversity and democracy of voices, in content and in form. Playwriting has the potential to offer authentic opportunities for students to grapple with 'big' ideas and develop a lasting proficiency that fosters symbolic and creative thinking. It encourages students to develop their reflective skills and increases self-knowledge while also encouraging a belief in their ability to contribute to and influence their culture and their world.

At a time when the need for greater understanding of ourselves and of each other is so pressing (Anderson, 2014), increased engagement with playwriting and its ability to encourage both empathy and personal growth seems a practice that deserves much greater attention.

The playwriting workshop approach also encourages 'actual' collaboration and community engagement in a time when contact with others is becoming increasingly virtual and mediated – a tyranny of digitalized artificial distance. The benefits of playwriting to our students has the long-term potential to contribute to more diverse and vibrant new performance writing, as well as the potential to encourage more engaged and culturally aware citizens, contributing to a more diverse, empathetic and vigorously democratic society.

However, the fundamental lesson from this book goes beyond playwriting, playwriting teaching and even drama education.

The major conclusion motivating this book is that I believe that creativity is the currency of the twenty-first century.

Therefore, teaching students how to understand, develop and mobilize their creativity will be as important as any knowledge we teach them – and perhaps as important as literacy and numeracy. Teaching for and about creativity is the best way to prepare our students for the volatile, ambiguous and complex future.

Luckily, creativity, as a process and an ability, is something that is freely available to all, independent of school resources or location. What it does need, though, is a teacher willing to teach with creativity, teach about creativity and, most importantly, teach for creativity. Teachers in the twenty-first century need to model, support, reward and expect creativity.

As drama teachers, this may seem to be a given. And while dispelling the myths about creativity in our own field may still be an unfinished assignment, these lessons need to be shared with all our students and, therefore, all our colleagues.[1]

Emphasizing the importance of creativity in the teaching and learning experiences of our students addresses two key challenges for all educators – engagement and agency: being invested in their learning and being aware of their capacity to influence and change their world. The approach outlined in this book – with its emphasis on skill and knowledge development – will help students develop a proficiency that encourages them to address the key challenges of their world. Its positive framework, emphasizing possibility thinking and play, fosters an environment that engages students in the teaching and learning experience – open, student-centred learning based on ideas of their choosing.

The stories we tell reflect who we are and who we think we are. Paraphrasing Freire (1974), unless we can encourage students to reimagine the world, they won't be able to recreate

---

[1] I recommend teachers interested in this possibility consult Jefferson and Anderson, *Transforming Schools: Creativity, Critical Reflection, Communication, Collaboration* (2017) for a detailed and inspiring discussion of how this might be done.

it or change it. And to generate creative and engaging teaching and learning experiences helps re-engage those students at risk of feeling school is not for them.

Rigorous and scaffolded creativity education, in this case through the lens of playwriting, will benefit students beyond the walls of the drama workshop space. The focus on possibility thinking, allowing students time to develop ideas, gather information and collaborate, models problem finding and problem solving applicable across disciplines. While it requires teacher explication and emphasis, this approach to creativity will help students develop Sawyer's (2012) concept of transference – that the skills, observations and understandings developed in one area can be applied in another, unrelated area. And these skills of transference are heightened through developing students' understanding of analogy – again, drama's emphasis on metaphor and symbol prepares students for key skills of creative thinking. It will strengthen young peoples' skills of creativity for life, in their world as much as in their career. It will bring them skills and understandings that will help them adapt to a world whose problems are complex and a future whose challenges are currently unknown.

References

Anderson, M. (2014). 'The Challenge of Post-normality to Drama Education and Applied Theatre'. *Research in Drama Education: The Journal of Applied Theatre and Performance*, 19(1), 110–20.

Freire, P. (1974). *Education for Critical Consciousness*. London: Sheed & Ward.

Jefferson, M. and Anderson, M. (2017). *Transforming Schools: Creativity, Critical Reflection, Communication, Collaboration*. London and New York: Bloomsbury Academic.

Sawyer, R. K. (2012). *Explaining Creativity: The Science of Human Innovation*. Oxford and New York: Oxford University Press.

INDEX